D1419164

Effective Fundraising

An informal guide to getting donations and grants

Luke FitzHerbert

DIRECTORY OF SOCIAL CHANGE

Published by
Directory of Social Change
24 Stephenson Way
London NW1 2DP
Tel. 08450 77 77 07; Fax 020 7391 4804
E-mail books@dsc.org.uk
www.dsc.org.uk
from whom further copies and a full books catalogue are available.

Directory of Social Change is a Registered Charity no. 800517

First published 2003

ISBN 1 903991 40 4

British Library Cataloguing in Publication Data
A catalogue record for this book is available from the British Library

Cover and text designed by Sarah Nicholson

Typeset, printed and bound by Stephen Austin, Hertford

Other Directory of Social Change departments in London:
Courses and conferences 08450 77 77 07
Charity Centre 08450 77 77 07
Charityfair 020 7391 4875
Publicity & Web Content 020 7391 4900
Policy & Research 020 7391 4880

Directory of Social Change Northern Office:
Federation House, Hope Street, Liverpool L1 9BW
Courses and conferences 08450 77 77 07
Policy & Research 0151 708 0136

Contents

About the series

Series editor: Alison Baxter

This series of starter guides is aimed primarily at those who are new to the voluntary sector. The series is designed for people involved with charities or voluntary organisations or community groups of any size. All the titles offer practical, straightforward advice to enable readers to get the most out of their roles and responsibilities.

Also available in this series:
The Charity Treasurer's Handbook
Gareth G. Morgan
2002
The Minute-taker's Handbook
Lee Comer and Paul Ticher
2002
The Charity Trustee's Handbook
Mike Eastwood
2001

For further information and to order books, please contact the Directory of Social Change (see page 83 for details).

About the author

Luke FitzHerbert, who works for the Directory of Social Change, is the founding editor of its *Guide to the Major Trusts* and *National Lottery Yearbooks*. He has been running DSC's courses on effective fundraising for 15 years.

Foreword

Over the last 15 years people from more than 2,000 organisations have come to the Directory of Social Change's basic courses on effective fundraising. This book is dedicated to them because it is based almost wholly on their experiences, which they have generously shared with the rest of us. In particular, of course, I thank those who have made specific contributions to the text.

During these years we have enjoyed a cascade of new statutory funding. Welcome though the money is, it also brings a threat to the independence of many charities. Government priorities may overlap with our own, but they will seldom be exactly the same. Only our own independent resources guarantee our ability to stick to our priorities, rather than those of our funders. Indeed I see our donated income, along with our use of voluntary donated time, as the core of what gives us our particular value and importance.

I hope this little book helps some of you to raise the money to fulfil some of your own dreams.

Luke FitzHerbert
November 2003

The Directory of Social Change thanks the Robert Gavron Charitable trust for its support for the writing of this book.

1 **The fundraising background**

Fundraising and other forms of funding

People use the word 'fundraising' differently, but in this book I am talking about persuading people or institutions to give donations to your charity. A donation is a gift – one that is normally made without the giver, or donor, expecting anything back in return, beyond the satisfaction of supporting what you do.

This book does not cover other ways of funding your work, either through contracts or agreements for the supply of your services, or by charging people for what you do. In such cases, there is no gift involved; your charity is 'selling' its services.

The book is about fundraising for charities (whether registered or not). It does not discuss raising money for the benefit of individuals, nor for private as opposed to public institutions such as, say, golf clubs or privately owned historic buildings. The box below explains what a charity is, and highlights the benefits of being registered as such.

Charitable status

If your organisation is non profit and for public benefit, it is likely to be a charity. If you have an income of £1,000 in a year or more, you should register with the Charity Commission if you are based in England or Wales – it is one of the country's silliest criminal offences not to do so, though fortunately this rule has never been enforced unless there has been some kind of misrepresentation (the rule is likely to be changed in the promised new Charities Act).

However there is no law to prevent you asking for money for a good cause – or indeed for any cause. You can get on with it without waiting for the formalities, though of course you must not say that you are a registered charity if you are not. You will just need to convince those you ask that what you are doing deserves their support.

However there are substantial advantages in being registered with the Charity Commission (or being recognised by the Inland Revenue in Scotland and Northern Ireland with a registration number to prove it. Registration as an Industrial or Provident Friendly Society comes to the same thing. Again, all this may change with a new Charities Act).

1 It is seen as a seal of respectability
In fact supervision by the Charity Commission is extremely light and, for charities with an income of under £10,000 a year (over half of all charities), it scarcely exists. Any investigations by the Commission are generally the result of outside complaint. However the Commission does require that properly audited or checked accounts are produced and it is beginning to demand proper annual reports as well.

2 You get Council Tax relief
Registered charities with their own premises get at least an 80% reduction on this tax – a very important saving.

3 You become eligible for tax reliefs on donations
These are described later in this chapter (page 9).

Some people and institutions, including many trusts and foundations, either can or will give their money only to registered charities. If you are too small to be registered, or have not yet got around to doing so, you will need to find a charity that is already registered to receive the donation or grant and then pass it on to you. This charity has to accept the responsibility for seeing that the money is indeed used for a genuinely charitable purpose. Various 'umbrella' charities are used to performing this function. They include many national associations and also local councils of voluntary service (CVSs). For details of these, go to www.nacvs.org.uk.

Should we fundraise for our charity?

Not necessarily. Donations or grants are just one way of funding what you do. Perhaps it would be more appropriate to charge for your work, like a charitable theatre company probably will. Maybe it makes more sense for your counselling service to be funded by a contract from one of the NHS's new Primary Care Trusts. Perhaps your national association of whatever would be best funded by subscriptions from member organisations in return for the services you give them. Perhaps, like my own organisation, DSC, you are best suited to being a trading organisation – in our case, selling books like this to you! It is perfectly normal and proper for charities to be trading organisations though, of course, any profits must stay within the organisation.

But if you think that donations are an appropriate source for some or all of your funding, go for it. There is no shortage of money and there are people out there only too happy to support almost every cause if you can identify them, if you have a good case and if you ask them nicely.

However if you, or a substantial proportion of your committee or trustees, have any doubts about it, perhaps you should not do it. If you would be embarrassed to be asked to support the cause yourself, then asking the public, let alone your family or friends, to pay for it will be uncomfortable and usually unsuccessful. No-one should fundraise unless they are convinced that what they are doing is proper and appropriate.

Aren't there easier ways of getting money?

Sometimes there may be, especially at the present time. Government, national, local or through the NHS, seems to be almost hurling money at many kinds of charity, with scheme after scheme calling for massive levels of voluntary sector participation. If you fit their priorities – which is likely if you are in a 'disadvantaged' area – you may well be able to get funding through one of their many 'partnerships'.

It will need a willingness to engage with the bureaucracy, but many people are very good at this, and some actually get a kick out mastering the procedures.

But where there is no other funding available you will have to fundraise; and even when there may be a choice, having at least a substantial proportion of your own fundraised income may be hugely desirable.

··

The Charity Commission register

There are over 180,000 registered charities and perhaps as many again that are not registered. Usually charities do not register because they are too small but sometimes they are exempt from registration, like universities and churches. (In Scotland and Northern Ireland there is, as yet, no Charity Commission, though organisations can register as charitable with the Inland Revenue to get access to charitable tax reliefs.) To get a feel for what is out there, why not try a browse through the Charity Commission register on its excellent website at www.charity-commission.gov.uk/registered charities? For a quick idea, you might go to 'Search the Register', choose 'Search by name' and 'Search by area', and enter the name of the place you live. You will probably be surprised by the number that show up. For example there are 25 charities that include the name of my home town of Totnes and 200 based in our local South Hams district.

What are the advantages of having fundraised income?

Having its own unrestricted income gives a charity its freedom and independence. Reliance on contracts or service agreements, or even on grants from just one or few government bodies, puts you very much in their power. And without independence, why be a charity in the first place? Would it not be more sensible just to work either for the public sector directly or as a business in the new and growing 'social economy'?

Is getting grants 'fundraising'?

For me, it depends on the conditions that come with the grant. If the grant comes as money for you to do what you want to do, sure. But when it is given on the basis of 'if you do the following, we will give you a "grant"', we are no longer talking about a donation to your charity but about a payment for your services, which is something different. Many grants fall in a grey area somewhere in between.

Caution!

Either way, be cautious. Experienced fundraiser Gerry Beldon puts it strongly: 'Grants are bad for us. We need them in the early stages of our projects, but we should plan from day one to develop alternative funding that is within our control'.

Fundraised money

Where does fundraised money come from?

No-one knows at all precisely. Such figures as exist are unreliable, largely because there are no central records and no two organisations seem to use the same definitions in the same way. Here is the best I can do, largely from figures published by the National Council of Voluntary Organisations (NCVO) and the Charities Aid Foundation (CAF) – www.ncvo-vol.org.uk and www.cafonline.org.

Sources of fundraised money

Individual donations and support	Over £4,000 million (of which legacies make up about £1,000 million)
Grants from central and local government	About £1,900 million
Grants from trusts and foundations, and other charities	About £1,200 million
Lottery grants (arts and heritage as well as health/welfare)	About £900 million
Sponsorship by companies (especially for arts)	About £430 million
Grants from companies	About £325 million

Note that this is the total of the money coming in, before subtracting the costs of getting it, which averages about 19p for every pound donated, though this figure varies greatly from charity to charity and from one kind of donation to another (see page 12).

How is the money given?

Most of it comes from individual donations, subscriptions or the sponsorship of fundraising events; as grants from trusts and foundations; or in grants or sponsorship from companies.

Individuals make donations while they are alive, as either single gifts or regular payments, in response to

- personal or telephone request and discussion
- letters (direct mail)
- advertising
- word of mouth
- taking part in your events.

Their money may come

- as single payments, usually by cheque
- as membership subscriptions

- as regular donations by direct debit or standing order
- through buying tickets to events or for lotteries
- from sponsoring your supporters' activities.

And it comes as legacies, through people's wills when they die.

Trusts and foundations, and some Lottery distributors, make grants to other charities, either from the income from their 'endowed' wealth or from money they have themselves raised from the public – BBC Children in Need and the like.

Central and local government give some free-standing grants to charities whose existence they value, though now they more often simply buy from charities specific services that they want to have provided.

Companies give grants to charities and may also sponsor your activities, usually in return for publicity or PR benefits for themselves.

Where else may it come from?

Some of the money recorded as donations probably comes through charity shops, gift catalogues and the like. These are often more akin to trading activities than to fundraising. They raise perhaps another £1,000 million, but are not covered by this book.

Don't believe everything you hear

To show the extraordinary uncertainty of figures about fundraising, the *United Kingdom Voluntary Sector Almanac 2002*, published by the NCVO, had the following two sentences on page 1:

'Donations from the general public accounted for £3.1 million.'

'The general public donated a total of £6.6 million to charity.'

One figure is based largely on a survey of charities asking how much they had received, the other largely from a survey of the public asking how much they had given. You can guess which figure is based on which source! But there are many other sources of uncertainty.

Why is the total of grants from companies so small?

Many people are surprised to find how little of the total comes as donations from companies. The reason is our old friend, spin. So much active publicity is given to even modest corporate donations, that it has created a general but false public impression that companies are a major source of donations. They are not. However because they are thought to be, many charities make quite unrealistic plans and offer equally unrealistic fundraising jobs in the area of 'corporate fundraising'.

How is the overall picture changing?

For the better. Each year more and more is being given to charities, in almost every way, even allowing for inflation. The only area which is reported to be actually going down is the contribution from companies. These are good times for fundraising, though it is also true that they are even better times for Britain as a whole – incomes have been rising even faster than charitable donations, especially the incomes of the better off. So there are more donations to come, if we ask correctly.

What causes do the public support?

The main causes receiving the money are (with very approximate figures)

Medical research	17%
Children or young people	14%
Religious organisations	13%
Overseas aid or relief	12%
Medical and health care	10%
Disabled, blind, deaf	8%
Elderly	3%
Homeless	3%
Heritage, environment	3%
Museums, arts	3%

However my heretical opinion is that lists like the one above do not necessarily reflect public preferences so much as they reflect the amount of fundraising expenditure in each field. People seem to give more because they are asked to, rather than because they wish to support this

7

charity rather than that. With almost £500 million being spent on charity fundraising each year, the distribution of this money between different fields may be the most important factor. If more was spent on fundraising for, say, homelessness then I would expect it to move up the table.

It is also interesting to see how much of the money goes to charities of different sizes.

Annual income of charities	% share of money fundraised
Less than £100,000	17%
£100,000 to £10 million	50%
Over £10 million	33%

Britain's favourite big charities

Voluntary donations in 2002:

Cancer Research UK	£239 million
Oxfam	£122 million
The National Trust	£118 million
Royal National Lifeboat Institution	£107 million
British Heart Foundation	£104 million

Note here a typical difficulty with such figures. Unlike donations to the other four charities, National Trust members' subscriptions include purchase of entry tickets to Trust properties as well as donations. Besides a warm glow of virtue, the donor also gets something tangible back.

What methods of giving are used by donors?

There are no very reliable figures but probably about one third of the money comes in some form of 'planned giving' such as regular donations or subscription payments and other substantial, tax-effective, one-off donations. Sponsorship and church collections – and look to churches, mosques, synagogues and so on to see effective fundraising in regular action – account for over 10% of the money fundraised. All the other methods, such as street or door-to-door collections and even radio and TV appeals, account for only a few per cent each at best.

Although there are very many small gifts, say of £5 or less, they account for only a tiny amount of the total donated – less than 3%. Over 60% of all the money is given in gifts of £50 or more. This should not surprise us: £50 is no longer a large amount for many, even most people; it is what it costs me to take my modest family out for a meal in a local pub.

Caution!
It is very difficult to raise substantial money from small, single 'pocket money' donations. Most charities have to think of asking people for significant amounts, or small amounts regularly repeated, similar to what they have to pay for just about everything else of any significance. Coins seldom play an important part in fundraising.

Tax reliefs

How can donations qualify for tax reliefs?

Everyone knows that gifts to registered charities can attract tax reliefs, but not many people understand how the system actually works. Some people even think that it is a racket by which rich people save money every time they make a big donation.

The principle is straightforward, even if the practice isn't. When a taxpayer (or tax-paying organisation such as most companies) gives money to a charity, the donor has already paid tax in order to have this amount available to give. This pre-paid tax can be reclaimed, making every £5 given worth something over £6 to the charity.

The main current scheme is called Gift Aid. To have, say, £100 to give, the donor will have paid £28 in income tax at the basic rate. The charity, with the donor's permission, can reclaim that £28 from the Inland Revenue. The charity ends up £128 richer while the donor is just £100 poorer than if the gift had not been made.

If the donor has also paid higher rate of income tax he or she will have had a further £23 already taken in tax. This too can be reclaimed, but this time by the donors themselves, through their end of year tax returns rather than by the charity. If this happens the charity will still end up with £128 but the donor will only be £77 out of pocket – generous stuff and one of the reasons why it makes sense to seek out prosperous donors whenever possible.

Note that companies can get similar tax benefits, but grants from trusts or from statutory organisations do not qualify as these are not taxpayers.

There are other tax concessions to do with payroll giving (see below) and with gifts of shares. In every case a first port of call for detailed information is likely to be the Giving Campaign (www.giving campaign.org.uk). They have a superb and downloadable Guide for Fundraisers.

Legacies to registered charities are also free of inheritance tax.

How important are these benefits?

No-one knows how much influence they have on people's decisions to give money to charities. My own view is that they are probably more important in generating additional money from donations that would have been made anyway than they are in persuading people to give in the first place.

How difficult is it to organise the tax reclaims?

For a charity with a permanent, stable finance or fundraising department, it is pretty simple, but that is not many of us. Otherwise consider using the agency service of CAF or of a few other similar providers. They will give you a quote and from then on, if you accept it, you just supply the information and the money will appear in your bank account.

Should a small charity like ours get involved?

Yes, if you are going to get significant donations from taxpayers. But you can probably wait until you have the first of them in hand.

Payroll giving

Payroll giving is another tax-effective way of making donations. Its promotion was my own first engagement with systematic fundraising – and it has not been all that successful. It is a system by which donors ask their employers for payments to the registered charity of their choice to be taken out of their pay each week or month.

How does it work?

To save each employer from having to send lots of small cheques to different charities every week or month, employers simply send one cheque for the total amount requested by all their employees to a clearing house – usually CAF, though there are others. CAF then reclaims the tax on all the money it receives each month and splits up the total among all the different charities that have been nominated (over 16,000 have been nominated so far).

How much is given?

Less than £100 million a year, which is only a couple of per cent of all donations.

Why is this disappointing?

Because payroll giving is such a big thing in the USA, with billions of dollars being given a year by this means, largely to local United Way organisations – which you may have come across under their former name of Community Chests, at least if you have ever played Monopoly.

Why has it not taken off over here?

I would ask the question the other way round – why has it been so successful in the USA? After all, it is just another technique for making payments, like cheques or standing orders. I believe its success in the USA is due to its connection with systematic local fundraising for a range of local needs, with everyone in every workplace being asked to contribute to sustain the work of local charities. Done during an annual community-wide autumn campaign, it is a brilliant idea. Unfortunately we have no equivalent in the UK.

Should our charity get involved?

Yes, simply by offering it to any donor as one of the ways of supporting your charity. However specifically targeting payroll gifts will often be worthwhile only if you can get access to a particular workforce and make a direct appeal to them – and this is a big 'if'. As there are many thousands of charities, companies can't realistically agree to let them all in, but you may have some special connection that can get them to open the door and, indeed, to support your appeal themselves. Local hospices, for example, might have a strong case with local employers – after all, they and their staff may well become beneficiaries of the hospice themselves in times to come. If you can get such privileged access, it is very well worth doing.

The costs of fundraising

How much does fundraising cost?

Hold onto your seat! Small charities, with all or most of their fundraising being done voluntarily, will often have low costs; perhaps less than 10% of the money raised (often a very different figure to 10% of the charity's total income). But in a bigger charity raising serious money from the general public, expect to pay an average of 30p in costs for £1 of income, unless:

- You are fundraising partly or entirely within a particular constituency with which you have a connection – say you are connected to a particular church, or are the local hospice.
- You get substantial legacy income, like, for example, the major cancer charities.

This 30p figure comes from a survey of the 250 largest fundraising charities, all with voluntary income of over £500,000 a year. The reason they are big, in many cases, is doubtless because they have been prepared to invest heavily in fundraising.

How much is it right to spend on fundraising?

Up to you. In some cases, where the need is great and no-one else is there to meet it, there might be little dispute about whether substantial costs are justified. The growth of the wonderful Medical Foundation for the Victims of Torture might be an example.

There are other cases where it can look as if a charity is attempting to expand beyond what its natural constituency can provide at a reasonable cost. If you find that every further pound you spend is struggling to bring in a fair return, perhaps the time has come to think again. To get a feel, look at the accounts of charities doing similar work to your own (they are obliged to send you a copy on request, and vice versa).

There are no clear rights or wrongs; just do what you think is right and explain both what you have done and why you have done it in your annual reports. But professional fundraising does work. Spend the money, with reasonable intelligence, and the rewards will normally come in.

The point about explaining what you have spent, and why, is one that has not been widely taken on board. Many of the largest charities fudge the presentation of their fundraising costs in their annual reports, or simply don't mention them at all, no doubt for fear of frightening their supporters (or the *Daily Mail*). I think they are taking an unwise risk.

2 Starting fundraising

Your fundraising strategy

You have to do three things. Together they make up what is called your fundraising strategy.

1 **Decide who is going to give your money**

Except for large charities you need names, or groups from which you will be able to get names, rather than generalisations (and this usually applies even when these people are working for big institutions – institutions cannot decide to sign cheques, only people within them can do this).

2 **Make sure these people know and like you and what you do**

Not much money is given to strangers. No matter how convincing your request, it is a weak start if the potential donor is actually thinking, 'who on earth are these people?'

3 **Ask them, repeatedly, for money**

Much the most productive fundraising is in the form of face-to-face or at least telephone requests. There are all sorts of ways of arranging for such requests to be made – at your events, ringing people you know, or 'at so and so's suggestion', indeed on every occasion you or your colleagues meet other people. Personal letters, and to a greater extent 'circular' mailings, rate second best. Other forms of advertising and the like generate little, though they may produce new leads to be approached more productively. But it is often helpful to soften the blow, by offering some modest inducement, such as a raffle or lottery ticket, or entry into a draw.

Who to ask for our money

Every charity is different and there is no simple answer. It will depend largely on the answers to the following questions.

Who is most likely to feel an interest in what you do?

This is your fundraising 'constituency' (though you may have a number of them). For example, the starting point for a charity like the Dystonia Society is likely to be people and families who have been affected by this medical condition; the Falkirk Preservation Society will probably be looking to civically minded citizens, probably a different though overlapping group to those who support the Falkirk Experimental Youth Theatre Group. The Karuna Trust, seeking support for Buddhist development projects in India, simply targets households in reasonably prosperous areas of any city, but this is much more challenging.

What resources do you have?

Your main initial resource is likely to be people. Look at yourselves. Your first need may be to recruit others to join your group. If you have determined and confident trustees, you may be able to raise money highly effectively by straightforward personal requests, as Joan Brander did for the Winged Fellowship, described in the following box. Or you may have people with experience and expertise in organising big fundraising events. You may have investors willing to finance the development of your fundraising. Or you may just be starting out as a small group of people on their own, with no resources and few contacts. This how most great fundraising charities started. They learned and grew by doing it.

The Winged Fellowship: from charismatic funder to professional fundraising

Without the drive and determination of charismatic founders, many charities would simply not be around today. Joan Brander is one such person. In the 1960s she was involved with a WRVS-inspired holidays scheme for disabled people. After hearing Joan's constant reflections on the inadequacy of services, her husband said 'Do something about it please!'

Joan became the founding trustee of Winged Fellowship Trust. She inspired people to donate cash, materials and labour, and the first Winged Fellowship holiday centre was born. Like most good ideas, it began to grow. Other centres emerged, led by local converts. Joan led the team by example, giving vast amounts of time.

The unpaid, committed, local pioneers complemented the drive, enthusiasm and belief systems of the founding trustee. The staff agenda became a mix of the cause and a burning need to do more, regardless of resources, because that was the example being set.

Autonomy grew and although the organisation provided broadly the same service at each location, local rules applied. The committed

---

needed the autonomy to get things done. This approach served the organisation well for quite some time. There seemed to be a global but unwritten mission statement. Unwritten, it was nevertheless in technicolour.

As the concept grew, more paid staff were recruited. Centres had to be professionally managed. Marketing became a requirement. As the need for more money arose, central office employed professional fundraisers to supplement a wealth of local fundraisers, often charismatic individuals themselves, recruited by Joan, who had an eye for spotting the talented, the caring and the committed.

By the mid-1990s Joan was no longer a trustee but she remained involved, having a personal manual database of long-standing committed donors. Joan would keep meticulous records of the hundreds of people she corresponded with. She knew when the son or daughter of a donor had a birthday; she always sent them a birthday card. But professionalisation was also required. Donors needed upgrading and staff required boundaries. No one person could replace Joan; it had to be the task of many in a complex and challenging environment.

The past five years have been filled with growing pains, though to change too quickly would destroy that innate passion injected by the founding trustee. Staff, both existing managers and rising stars, needed to be shown new ways of working to gain a more corporate sense and they began to work to collective standards. Clearer guidelines for local supporters were drawn up. For example, it's OK to have a local bank account but you must go through the charity to open an account in its name, provide returns and not disturb the organisation's revenue streams while still purchasing what the organisation needs.

On the way there were casualties. Some could not work in such an environment. 'Are we losing our spontaneity?' was a common cry, but overall the passion and commitment laid down by Joan Brander is a lasting legacy today.

Pat Wallace
Winged Fellowship

Do you need 'good' money or will 'bad' money do?

This may seem a silly question but it is not. For most charities there is 'good' money and not so 'good' money. The best money has two characteristics:

- it is free for you spend as you think best (general donations);
- it has the potential to be ongoing, year after year (regular, committed donors, or replicable fundraising events, say).

Not so 'good' money:

- is for one specified purpose only (so-called 'restricted funds');
- is short term rather than renewable (one-off or 'project' grants).

At present there is an absurd mismatch in the availability of the two kinds of money. The not so good, short-term project grants have never been so relatively easy to get, while the regular ongoing funding is as hard work as it ever was. This has tempted many charities into over-expansion on the basis of short-term grant funding. Then, after a few happy years, such funders move on, and the charity is left hanging in the air. The people who give these grants, usually government (local or national), the Lottery or trusts and foundations, are sometimes accused of 'funding to fail'. Few of them will support your charity's efforts to develop a sustainable flow of fundraised income.

Getting known

How do we get future funders to know and like us, and what we do?

This depends entirely on who you have decided to raise your money from. The key is to have a planned (and budgeted) programme to make your charity well known to these people.

Different target groups will need quite different approaches. As one example, think about the following strategy for those seeking grants from local authorities:

Developing or keeping grant support from a local authority

Start out with a clear idea of what you want and how you are going to get it:

- decide on a budget – perhaps 2.5% of the intended grant?

- identify all those in the authority who might have some influence on how your work is seen – perhaps about 100 names of councillors and officers from a number of departments, including the treasurer's and the PR people, and prepare address labels for all of them
- set up a programme for each of these people to receive or see something positive about your charity at least once a month – invitations, newsletters, press cuttings, Christmas cards or whatever (cheap to do in local authorities who will distribute materials internally free of charge)
- towards the decision date for the grant, begin a programme to lobby the key players, informally or formally – a drink in the pub with your chair may be just as good as a formal meeting in the civic offices.

In other situations, use other methods. The box below has two more quite different, but real examples from my own family's experience of small new charities putting themselves on the map for those on whose future support they would rely.

The Brent River Society

This was (and is) wholly local, seeking support from environmentally concerned citizens. 'Events' were an important means of getting publicity, the biggest of which was called the Grand Opening of the Brent River Park. The local authority had offered to contribute some hundreds of pounds to our project. The Society persuaded them to use it to buy the oak for about thirty new footpath signposts to be constructed and carved by local secondary schools. They were then unveiled by the Mayor in a four-mile procession, led by a volunteer pipe band and followed by a large crowd. The Society must have reached thousands, for minimal expenditure by the local authority, and none by itself.

The National Pyramid Trust

This was quite different. It was set up to establish preventive volunteer-led therapy groups for primary schoolchildren at risk of educational failure. The plan was for the groups, once established, to be funded out of local educational budgets but to seek funding from trusts and foundations for the development work of getting these local schemes set up.

Once the relevant trusts had been identified, the people concerned, along with senior people involved with such issues from universities and government departments – the 'stakeholders', to use the jargon – were invited to a briefing, followed by lunch, just 'to discuss with us our plans for taking the work forward'. The event had credibility because it was hosted for the charity by a foundation, the Gulbenkian. Though not itself big enough to become a major funder, Gulbenkian was and is recognised as expert in this kind of work.

No money was asked for at the meeting, but many hundreds of thousands of pounds followed in due course from the trusts that had got to hear of Pyramid at that early stage – even those who did not come to the briefing – (and, eventually, the ongoing funding for all the pilot projects was indeed generated from local sources).

Your case for funding

Why should people give you their money?

Before you start asking your target people for money, you should be clear about your 'case'. This is not so much because you will meet with many difficult questions but because unless you yourselves are clear and confident about your case, you will not come across convincingly to others.

This case will have two different parts:

- First, you will show that there is a real, urgent and important need for what you do or are proposing to do.
- Second, you will show that yours is a well-organised and impressive organisation which they can trust to use their money well.

In the DSC Effective Fundraising course, we use the check list of possible 'selling points' set out in the box below. Most charities should be able to point to about eight of the ten.

What are your main selling points?

About your work

- **The urgency or the extent of the problem of need**
  If you don't think it is really important, why should anyone else? But it does not have to be more important than other causes – we need

both ballet and an end to child cruelty.

- **Its emotional or sympathetic appeal**
  Donations are more about liking than thinking, so this is usually
  essential. It is therefore hard to get donations for charities that are away
  from the front line, like national associations, or councils of voluntary
  service (but they may have particular projects with greater appeal).

- **Its innovations**
  Charity is always with us, but any convincing new approach, or just a
  new element in an existing approach, is attractive.

- **Its cost effectiveness**
  Can you offer a lot in return for the money, perhaps through the
  involvement of volunteers? If so, make the point. If not, talk about
  something else.

- **Its value as an investment for the future**
  Will their donation live on doing good for years, or will you just be
  back for more for the same need for the same people next year?

- **The unhappy consequences if your work was to stop**
  Be careful that this does not come across as a whine. 'The children
  will starve and it will be your fault' is not a successful approach.

About your organisation

- **Its appearance of excellence**
  Everything about you, from your telephone manner to your
  letterhead and your annual report should be better than expected
  for a charity of your kind – and all this without looking expensive
  either! This means hard work (and money, but you should be able to
  get a small grant for this if you need it. See page 74)

- **Its independent endorsements**
  If you are wonderful, as all DSC readers' organisations are, you will
  be able to get endorsements from people known to the donors, at
  least by reputation, and with no axe to grind, who will say 'these
  people are really pretty good'.

- **Its record of previous successes**
  'Success breeds success' and 'to them that hath shall more be given'.
  If you have had successes, make sure they show. If not, can you
  quote the successes of others whose lead you are following?

- **The strength of its voluntary input**
  Most donors like the 'voluntary' part of the voluntary sector. All

charities have volunteers (its trustees, if no others) so have them up front when fundraising – (it's where they belong).

- **Its community support**
Are you one of those single-minded, almost crazed fanatics who have been responsible for building up most of our greatest charities? Good for you if you are, but hide it for fundraising purposes as it can deter donors who prefer to see a widely based movement.

How do I get across the need for our work?

The basic appeal is best if it is simple:

'People with this condition need help and support and they are not getting it.'

'Because of us, children living on the street in Brazil get proper lives.'

'Our town looks a mess. Let's sort it out.'

'There are people here, looking after disabled family members, who never get a holiday or a break.'

'Help fight asthma.'

'Give everyone the chance of a decent and dignified death.'

'We must bring on a new generation of young musicians.'

'Help lonely old people get together at our weekly lunch clubs.'

... and then?

1 Don't give more detail, give examples instead. Donors give money when they are moved far more often than when they are convinced. And what moves people is the particular example, far more than the persuasive argument. See the box below for a good example from Oxfam. And remember that, if you can't talk to the donor personally, then a picture is indeed worth a thousand words.

2 Say, very briefly, how you organise the work – we fund researchers, organise volunteer respite carers, or whatever. Only elaborate if asked. Donors tend to be much more interested in the people or situation that you are addressing than in the mechanics of how you do it.

Caution!

Some people get very worked up about language. You may have noticed that in this book I occasionally use words like 'old' rather than 'elderly', and so on. Donors have rights too and we must steer a middle course between the language that we prefer within our own organisations and that which donors use in their daily lives. To insist on using our professional phraseology, even when it will serve to put off the very people who we are seeking to recruit to the cause, seems as patronising as the other way round. Resist being bullied into exaggerated political correctness.

We all use jargon when it is useful internally or when dealing with others in our field, but we can avoid it when talking – let alone writing – to donors. 'Outreach', 'BME', 'task centred', 'ESF', 'outcome based', 'key stage' and 'service provision' were some examples mentioned when I briefly floated this thought with a group of foundation folk. Even apparently commonplace words or phrases like 'beneficiaries', 'line management', 'housing benefit', 'therapy', 'human resources' or 'advocacy' are best either avoided or explained.

Oxfam

Oxfam, with an income of over £100 million a year, does almost every kind of work in almost all parts of the world. How do you put this in less than 200 words? This is the text of one of their general purpose fundraising leaflets (half the space on the leaflet is taken up by a picture of Alamru, the boy described).

> *Save lives by giving Oxfam £2 a month*
> In Alamru's village, in a dry, barren area of Ethiopia, water is scarce. In the past, the little water that people had was dirty and unsafe. Too often, Alamru watched friends – both young and old – fall ill. The villagers needed water to live, and yet with each drop they risked lethal diseases, like cholera and diarrhoea.
>
> Alamru and his fellow villagers wanted to end this terrible threat to their lives. They knew that all they needed to save lives was a supply of cleaner, safer water. They also knew that they could ask Oxfam for help in building their own well. After weeks of digging, Alamru was the first to strike water. Now the whole village has clean safe water and far fewer young children fall ill. How can just £2 a month do all this?

The answer lies in the way Oxfam works alongside poor people to help them find solutions that will last into the future. For example, in Alumru's village it was the villagers themselves who dug the well, who installed the pump, and who will maintain it for the future. Oxfam helps by providing expert know-how and by providing the tools that poor people just don't have.

What about reasoned argument?

It has its place, but its use in fundraising is often indirect. The best way to demonstrate your credibility, when fundraising, is not by argument but by endorsement. Use your arguments to persuade the right people to endorse your work (the right people are those who enjoy the respect or affection of your potential donors).

For example, a personal recommendation by Bob Geldof, based on personal knowledge of its work, might be extremely valuable to a small overseas aid charity; so might the endorsement by the local football club manager for your scheme for a new youth club; or by the lord lieutenant of the county for your town festival; or by the chair of the county law society for your new legal advice idea. In all cases, the people concerned will be putting their own reputations on the line, so they will need to be convinced of the good sense of your project.

Many organisations benefit greatly from the endorsement and support of celebrities. Just look at the example of Princess Diana and land mines. But media celebrity can backfire; and you should not have to pay.

Caution!

For fundraising purposes, it is usually unproductive to try to persuade people who are not on your side already. For example, if someone assumes that most asylum seekers are scroungers, just ask someone else less prejudiced. There are nearly always plenty of well-disposed people out there only too happy to support you if they are asked. You may well want to convert the sceptical for all sorts of other excellent reasons, but don't expect it to raise much money.

Artangel

The most unlikely causes find supporters. I remember a long time ago someone from Artangel, a performance art charity, trying to persuade the other members of a DSC training course that shrink-wrapping

Nelson's Column in plastic, in the name of art, was something that people should donate to. There was polite but general derision. However two people, too shy to dissent in public, told me afterwards that they thought that this was one of the most exciting projects that they could imagine. And Artangel has become a most successful fundraising charity – though I don't think they ever got to Nelson.

What makes a strong case for funding?

You need to be able to give clear, consistent and uncomplicated answers, at a range of levels, to the question 'why do you need my money?' Many potential funders will only want to talk at one of these levels, but you must be prepared to meet them at the level they choose, which could include

- your vision and mission – why you exist
- your long-term goals
- your immediate objectives
- your financial needs.

The box below gives an example.

Blankshire Children's Society

Vision and mission
Children brought up 'in care' have poor life prospects, often because they have missed out on their education and so have low levels of literacy.

This is largely avoidable. These children deserve as good an education as other children, but they often don't get it, usually through no fault whatsoever of their own. We exist to change this situation.

Goals
We want every child 'in care' in Blankshire to have the same level of personal support for their education that we would expect for our own children.

Second, we want the County Council to take the issue far more seriously. At present they have no idea how these children are doing at school.

Immediate objectives
First we intend every child to have a permanent, voluntary adult 'mentor' for their education, who will stay with them as they move

from foster home to foster home or whatever. Through their mentor they will have the same consistent encouragement and support, in both term time and holidays, as other children.

Second, we will persuade the County Council to keep and publish figures on the educational progress of the children in its care, so that this can be monitored and action taken where necessary.

Financial needs
The mentor programme
We need to support 18 existing mentors supporting 48 children this year and we intend to recruit, train and have in place six more mentors.

The annual cost of the existing service is £24,000, or £750 a child, funded by the donations of our supporters. The support of six new mentors will mean a further £8,000 a year is needed (their recruitment and training will be funded by grants from foundations).

The campaigning programme, to influence the County Council, is carried out by our voluntary committee members but we have budgeted £4,000 to give them the office support they need.

A copy of the detailed budgets is available on request.

How do we fundraise for 'core' salaries or administrative and overhead costs?

In a word, don't. Raising money for things like this is not easy. Fortunately, it is also not necessary.

The general rule is to raise money for what you do, not for the costs of doing it. Almost all charities are doing work that is attractive to donors, providing it is brought to their attention. Donors are seldom interested in any breakdown of the costs in doing so. If it costs you £10,000 every year to bring 15 sick children from Chernobyl for a holiday in Britain, they will decide that this is good value, or not, without usually being interested in how much of it is salaries, how much air fares and so on. After all, when you buy a loaf of bread, do you worry about the administration costs of the shop, or the levels of staff salaries in the bakery? You are only interested in what you get for your money. So it is with most donors.

Trusts and foundations may well be interested in your budgets, but this is usually just to satisfy themselves that you are properly organised and are therefore likely to achieve what you have promised to achieve – which is what they are funding. (The people who really are obsessed with the details of your costs are local authorities and other public bodies, whose excessive attention to such issues derives from historical concerns about the misuse of public money. This approach is deeply counter-productive as far as getting good value from the services they fund is concerned. Other donors not only do not share their attitudes, but are often actively hostile to them – as you would probably be yourself.)

But money for salaries or administration is what we actually need!

Let me try again – this is really important! It is not your organisation that the money is needed for. It is needed for the work that you do. You do not have to say 'in order to pay my salary, please give me £20,000' when you could say 'in order for these unfortunate children to have their holiday, please give me £20,000'. This is not trickery. It is actually the accurate and proper approach. Look at the following example, showing two ways of presenting the same costs (for a fictitious and simplified community centre).

Core costs and overheads: an example

Worton Community Centre

A 2004 Costs

Salaries	£30,000
Rent	£ 8,000
Office costs, telephone etc.	£ 6,000
Repairs and renovations	£ 6,000
Total	£50,000

B 2004 Costs

Drop-in centre	£ 8,000
Lunch clubs	£14,000
Youth club	£18,000
Holiday programme	£10,000
Total	£50,000

Note that both lists are recording the same money. The first list shows what the money was spent on, the second shows what it was spent for. (Note also that the second way of putting it, not the first, is the one expected by the Charity Commission in a charity's accounts, with the first being just an optional extra for the 'Notes').

Is it easier to ask for money for the things in List A or in List B? The answer is obvious, but we still find charity after charity asking for money for the rent or the phone bill or the salary or whatever when they could be raising it for the old people or the youngsters who need your club.

What if my work doesn't break down into easy bits?

There are many ways of breaking down the costs of your work that do not involve headings like salaries or rent. Here are some examples, where the salaries and so on simply do not appear.

- The cost per activity – as in the example above: 'The youth club in our centre costs £18,000 a year'.
- The cost per beneficiary – your total costs divided by the number of people you help: 'Our training programme costs £250 for each trainee'.
- Cost per location – your total costs divided among the areas where you work: 'Our service in Alloa costs £2,000 a year, in Falkirk £3,000'.
- Cost per event – ideal for many arts groups: 'Our performance of *Hamlet* in Cardiff prison in January will cost £4,000, of *As you Like It* in Belmarsh in June, £3,000.
- Cost per day, week or month – your total cost divided by 365, 52 or 12. We can all do this: 'We need 52 sponsors for our Keep Doncaster Clean programme'.
- Cost per achievement – your total cost divided by the number of successes achieved: 'It costs £30 to get each child through its bicycling test'.

What if someone wants to know about our salaries, rent and so on?

You have nothing to hide, so just tell, them, but these are unlikely to be the most important things they need to know. When approaching a possible donor, concentrate on saying what could be achieved with their money; everything else is secondary and subsidiary. A number of trust administrators have said to me that applicants assume that they are primarily interested in the old-fashioned cost breakdown, 'but why on earth should we be?'

Is this the new 'outcome funding' approach?

Yes, except that it is not a new approach at all. However the Lottery's Community Fund, many government programmes, a number of trusts and at least one adviser to major donors are re-emphasising it at present – and about time too. The bad example of the government practice of paying for services rather than for the results of such services had infected not only other funders, but also many applicant organisations. We had got used to asking local authorities for grants for salaries and so on.

There has been a big and generally welcome reaction. Now, more and more, we are rightly being asked 'what will we achieve?' if they give us the money, instead of 'what will we do?'

There is even a danger now of an excessive swing the other way. How will you measure the beneficial outcomes of replacing the clapped out drains in your residential home, and so on?

Some danger signs that funders look out for

Experienced funders are often on the look out for some of the more common potential danger signs:

- organisations which do not give the impression of being in control financially
- an organisation which is run by its staff with the trustees effectively sidelined
- an organisation where the fundraising applicant seems separated and distant from the work being done
- people raising money for their own activities that are not fully integrated into the rest of the organisation's work.

Isn't more detail needed for grant applications?

For applications for small amounts (say up to one or two thousand pounds) to small trusts, and unless their guidelines say otherwise, a simple request for £x with which to achieve your results is usually enough (when accompanied by a decent annual report and accounts).

For big grants you will often need to put in a more formal 'funding application', perhaps even with business plans and so on. Many trusts making such grants specify in some detail what they want. (See the section of this book on grant applications, page 66.)

But a full, formal 'funding application' for smaller projects can actually put off many donors, even institutional ones, who just want to support a good cause when they are asked nicely and with feeling. They may well feel irritated by being treated as an office with 'procedures' and 'requirements' when they want to think of themselves simply as concerned and benevolent individuals. Send only what they ask for; you can always say you have the full 42-page business plan if they want it.

Putting your case – an example

Here is an example of an exercise from our Effective Fundraising training course.

Suppose that you have had the following letter:

> My mother has recently died and in her will she asked me to give £10,000 to a charity of my choice. I am asking four organisations, of which yours is one, to give me a ring and say what you could do with a gift like this.

Prepare your call in reply to this – I suggest a one-minute maximum to start with – quite a long time on the phone.

The following examples (from Age Concern Blankshire) show two ways of approaching this, with most people's starting effort being something very like A:

Response A
I am ringing from Age Concern Blankshire in response to your letter. Is this a convenient time to speak?

First, Age Concern is very sorry to hear of your mother's death. Please accept the charity's condolences.

You ask about our work. Age Concern Blankshire was founded in 1937. In the first 30 years we concentrated on our volunteer driver scheme to help people who had not got, or couldn't use transport of their own, and indeed this is till running. Now, we support elderly people and their carers throughout the area in many different ways and we have grown until we have 27 professional staff on a range of projects – as well as lots of volunteers. Our services range from day centres and lunch clubs to advice surgeries and referral schemes. We also have a big outreach project as well as running a money advice clinic.

We are partly funded by the local authority, and a few of the projects bring in some of their own income, but we are always short of money and your mother's £10,000 would be an enormous boost and would of course be recognised in our next annual report.

I hope you will agree that this would make really good use of your mother's legacy.

This is more about your organisation than about your beneficiaries. It is also dry and impersonal, partly in the third person rather than the first, and uses jargon words like 'referral' and 'outreach'. Compare it with the following.

Response B
I am ringing from Age Concern Blankshire in response to your lovely letter. Is this a good time for us to talk?

First, I am very sorry to hear of your mother's death. Please accept our condolences. Did she know us?

So, what could we achieve with £10,000? Can I give you a couple of examples? Take our money advice scheme, because many elderly people are driven mad trying to cope with housing benefit and so on. Just yesterday, for example, Mrs Smith, who is housebound, told us she thought she was going to be evicted because her housing benefit claim was 'invalid', but she couldn't find out what was wrong with it because they just never called her back. Quite easy for us to clear up but a desperate worry for her – and she's 87! This whole service costs us less than £20,000 a year to run so your mum's £10,000 would help a whole lot of people like her!

Or would she have been more interested in our lunch clubs and drop-in centres? Loneliness is awful when you are old and we can do a great deal about it. And it's not expensive as they are mainly run by the old people themselves.

But may I ask you, what do you think your mother would have been most interested in?

This is much better, though my own preference would be neither of the above, just 'We do all sorts. Can you tell me what your mum was interested in and why you put us on your list?'

How do I show that our organisation is first class of its kind?

Here are some ideas.

1   You will be judged by appearances so it is a very great help to have printed materials that are seriously impressive for the kind of

organisation you are (without them looking expensive). Check:

- **The design of your letterhead and the quality of the paper** – photocopy quality is not usually good enough.

- **The appearance and style of your letters** – wide margins, no spelling mistakes or other careless errors, simple clear English, sounding like a letter from a charity not a business.

- **Your leaflets and newsletters** – do not try to save money by amateur design, and do not have too many words. Keep them short, simple and strong. Longer is usually worse, in fundraising terms. Often the pictures are central with only a very few words needed to explain them – and a very few big pictures are far better than lots of small ones.

- **Your annual report and accounts** – is this a document of powerful conviction or just a few word-processed pages pinned together?

And if all this seems too expensive, get a small grant specifically to enable you to present yourselves properly in public. There is a list of sources of small grants on the DSC website (www.dsc.org.uk).

2   Obtain short 'endorsement letters' from people, independent of your organisation and with no axe to grind, saying how good you are (I assume that you are pretty good, of your kind).

3   Ensure that everyone fundraising for your organisation is fully briefed and obviously committed to the work of the charity.

3 Getting donations from individuals

The most recent figures suggest that over £4 billion was given to charities by individuals in 2002. Sixty per cent of this was in gifts of £50 or more. Most of this is 'good' money, given for the work of the charity as a whole. A quarter or so comes in legacies and about another quarter is the very best money of all – regular donations or subscriptions, usually by bankers order or direct debit and set to continue 'until further notice'

Basic principles

What are the stages in raising money from individual donors?

1   **Acquisition** – getting the first donation, hopefully with the means of contacting donors again.

2   **Retention** – keeping them as regular or at least occasional donors.

3   **Development** – encouraging them to give more, or more often.

In practical terms the three stages come in this order, but in financial terms it is usually the other way round – more money will usually come from going back to existing supporters or contacts than from finding new ones. It is a common mistake for established charities to neglect those they already have in favour of an all-consuming search for new donors.

How can donors be approached?

Most fundraising charities use a combination of the following:

- Direct mail
- Sponsored activities
- Fundraising events
- Door-to-door collections
- Lotteries, raffles, games
- Personal solicitation (just asking).

Just asking, whether face-to-face or on the telephone, is probably the most important in financial terms for very many charities, but it is also a bit alarming for many people starting on fundraising, so we will leave it for the moment and come back to it later. But don't forget, if you need money, the easiest, quickest way to get it is to ask for it directly. (I don't count writing a letter as 'asking' in this context.) The box below shows how different approaches can be combined, and can develop over time.

St Luke's Hospice

The hospice is in Plymouth, a former dockyard city, with not much tradition of philanthropy, but a strong sense of community.

It was founded by a group of people, none of them particularly well off, centred on a church in the city centre. It took them five years of personal community fundraising of every kind to be able to buy their first house – with 7 bedrooms all upstairs and no lift. When they opened, the freshly recruited medical staff was warned first, that they would all have to do a bit of everything – fundraising as well as washing up – and second, that they only had enough money to pay the wages for three weeks!

Now, 21 years later, it has a purpose-built building and a staff of 125, many of whom still contribute to the fundraising, though there is now a substantial and professional fundraising team as well.

Particularly interesting is that it has developed a body of 11,000 regular supporters, contributing £1 a week each – or £52 a year. But they are not, at least on the surface, giving donations at all. They are buying lottery tickets and the chance to win a top prize of £1,000 each week (out of a £1,500 prize fund). However, quite simple maths will show that, as a gambling proposition, this is not too much of a catch and most of the money goes directly to the running costs of the hospice – with which everybody concerned seems to be entirely happy. But as the hospice explains, Plymouth people 'seem to prefer to support us in this way'. In fact, they say, relatively few people see themselves as 'donors'. Even those giving larger amounts often see this more as an appropriate payment for the services provided – or, perhaps, for services to be provided in the future. It is all wholly dependent on the hospice being accepted as the community asset it is.

Recently a young woman committed herself to raise £1,500 for the hospice, as well as all her own costs, as part of an expedition to climb Mount Kilimanjaro in Africa. In fact, after she achieved her target she went on sending in more money. When asked where she got this fundraising enthusiasm, she explained that she wasn't actually doing any fundraising at all. She just told everyone she met about the project 'and people just wanted to chip in'. But as the professional fundraiser pointed out, this was only because the passionate commitment of those involved with the hospice had come to be generally recognised, across Plymouth. And keeping that sense of passion, now that they had become a large and professional organisation, rather than the 'almost a commune' of the early days, would be their main challenge for the future.

Direct mail

What is direct mail?

This is the term used for sending fundraising letters by post to people listed on your 'donor base'. Though the letter may be a one-off appeal, each mailing is usually part of a regular organised mailing programme. Many readers may already be on the receiving end of such programmes – could you discuss what you get with your colleagues, to decide what approach suits you best?

How do I get a donor base?

You probably have one already, even if it only has the small number of people involved in setting up your organisation. You then build on this by every means possible:

- asking everyone you meet if they would like to be kept in touch with what you do;
- asking people for the names of other people you might write to;
- collecting names and addresses at your events;
- generating publicity that prompts people to approach you;
- swapping lists with other organisations (called reciprocal mailings and generally a good thing to do);
- buying lists – trickier.

How many people might we have on our donor base?

It varies from charity to charity. But it is as easy to have too many as too few. And if you invest one year on expanding your database, you must be willing to be quite ruthless in cutting it back again if the money is not coming in.

Is it alright to put our clients or their families on our mailing list?

Sure, unless there are some very special circumstances. If they themselves are unlikely to have the resources to be significant donors, you can ask if they have relatives or friends that might be happy to support you.

Won't I need more than one list?

You will probably quickly find that you need to 'code' your list because different people will need to get different letters (this is called segmentation). A starting division might be:

- **the hot list** – these are your active supporters and donors;
- **a warm list** – for those who in some way show interest in what you do: 'Thanks for coming to our bring and buy sale yesterday. Can we interest you further ...?';
- **cold lists** – for people who don't yet know you: 'As a local resident, can I interest you in ...?

How do I manage our lists?

A perfectly adequate database now comes as part of the 'package' with most computers. It will keep all the information you need and print out labels for you. You will need to keep, as a minimum, for each person:

- name and address
- the date and amount of all donations
- space for notes.

Very soon, if not immediately, you will find yourself also wanting:

- telephone numbers
- e-mail addresses
- date and nature of previous mailings/contacts.

The Directory of Social Change (publishers of this book) also publishes *Building a Fundraising Database Using Your PC* (details at www.dsc.org.uk). For larger charities, there are specialised donor-base packages available. Expert advice on them should be available through membership of the Institute of Fundraising (www.institute-of-fundraising.org.uk) or the excellent commercial site www.fundraising.co.uk.

How do we keep our lists up to date?

By unremitting hard work. We all get annoyed by inaccurate and out-of-date mailings. So you have to work out and constantly review exactly how you are going to keep yours accurate.

Furthermore it is not just accuracy but also good management that is needed. You probably have a few very important supporters, for example. How are you going to make sure that they do not get the same letters as the person who has given you £5? Managing your donor base calls for continuous intelligent effort – it is not a mere administrative routine to be delegated to whoever you can find.

In charities with a donor base of any size I would suggest giving one trustee the responsibility for keeping an eye on the quality of your mailing lists on behalf the trustees as a whole. It is that important.

Should we have a 'membership' or' friends' scheme?

Some charities are set up as membership organisations in the first place; others choose to introduce some kind of membership scheme. These may be useful but one word of warning. For some people, a membership subscription carries an image of a much lower payment than that of a straight donation, and is often related to what you get back for it – like being a member of a golf club. This may not be appropriate for your situation.

There is nothing wrong with just having supporters.

The Brent River Society mailing list

This Society, wholly voluntary, was set up by myself, my wife and a small group of others to get the local authorities to create a linear park along four miles of the River Brent in west London. The idea grew out of one of the activities of a previously existing preservation society, so there was a core of a couple of dozen people already involved from the start. It was (and is) a membership organisation and the membership grew to almost 2,000 in just a few years, mainly through local publicity, centred on maps of the proposed park in the local paper and on public meetings. At these meetings everyone was asked from the platform to consider joining the Society and was then invited to do so personally at the door as they left.

A particular success was an invitation to sign a protest petition – the

London County Council was proposing to put our nice river into a concrete trough. Everyone who signed also put their address – otherwise the signatures would carry no weight – and they were told that they would also be kept up to date with the outcome of the campaign. Hey presto! Several hundred new warm names on our mailing list.

Another interesting feature was (and is) the size of the subscription. Because campaigning was the first purpose of having the mailing list, with fundraising secondary, we wanted as many names as possible. We therefore set the subscription at '50p, or what you can afford'. Not only was no-one deterred by the cost, but also many people were embarrassed to give so little – 50p obviously didn't cover even the cost of posting the newsletters three times a year. In practice our average subscription rapidly rose to over £5 a head – and this was nearly 30 years ago in a far from rich part of London.

Can I swap a mailing list with a similar organisation?

Yes, charities do this and it usually works. The total given to the combined charities will be more than the two get separately. Some people feel that their lists should be guarded with their lives, and never shared. This feeling generally comes from a misapprehension about your supporters. There are actually only a few who will just support you and will not support other similar organisations. And getting a letter from another organisation is not a reason to stop supporting you anyway.

What about the Data Protection Act?

I have read the books on this (one published by ourselves) and remain pretty mystified. It seems to me that if your supporters will feel miffed about what you have done, it is probably illegal (though I have never heard of any charity, let alone a small one, getting into any trouble on this unless they have done something obviously out of order – like selling names to a commercial sales organisation).

However, if you are contemplating list swapping and want to know you are completely in the clear, just make sure you tell people in advance what you are doing – generally a desirable approach anyway. So why not say in your fundraising leaflets that you do this, with an opt-out box? I have used 'We share our list of supporters with partner charities in this field. If you do not want this, please tick here'.

What should we send in our mailings?

You should keep it as close as possible to a personal letter, together with the essential reply card or similar. This, if done well, will seldom be taken as 'junk mail'. You may also include printed material as back-up. For very large organisations, it may be impossible to be convincingly personal, and other approaches may be needed, but that will not apply to most readers of this book.

Specifically,

- Your letter can actually be personal in many cases, not just appear to be so. One individual can probably 'top and tail' 100 letters in an hour – so three trustees could do 600 letters in an evening, with the date, salutation and signature all done by hand (and with some of them having a personal PS at the bottom).
- There must be a response mechanism. Results are much affected by how easy it is to respond to your letter. The ideal will have a telephone number to ring with a credit card donation – hard for a small charity to arrange – and also a card and envelope with as much as possible pre-printed. For example, a standing order instruction where all the donor has to do is write in an amount and the name of their bank will get some donors who would otherwise not get round to finding their chequebook. Carefully consider using Freepost.
- Offering an opportunity to donate through your website is on the way, but so far seems to be most effective for media or e-mail-based appeals.
- You can enclose leaflets and so on, but they are inherently impersonal. If you do, try to connect them with your letter: 'I enclose a leaflet which has a nice picture of Mrs Smith on the inside', or whatever.

What should our letters say?

Almost anything can work if it is done nicely, but if you want some specific advice, try this:

1   The letter should say what a donation can do and should ask for the money to do it. '£10 a month can keep a child in our school who could not otherwise be in school at all.' I think this is better than 'Every year our supporters, and we hope you will become one of them, enable more than 150 severely disabled people, and their carers, to have a proper holiday'.

2   And then 'Can you send us a standing order – there is a pre-printed form on the back of this letter – or a cheque for whatever you can afford, in the attached envelope?' It is essential that your letter is

absolutely clear about what you are asking for. There is nothing wrong with starting out 'Can you give us a donation of £x so that ...'.

3   You may offer an inducement. 'All subscribers will be offered two free tickets to our annual ball' (at which they will be invited to take part in the tombola, patronise the bar and the supper tent) for example.

4   It is very important that if the person is already a supporter this is fully, accurately and properly recognised.

How long should the letter be?

Up to you. What would you like to get yourself? There is a big difference between a letter and other enclosures. A letter is asking to be read through to the signature at the end. The attachments are for them to read in detail only if they want to. Try your letters out on people not connected with your charity. But unless it is genuinely interesting, a long letter is less likely to be read than a short one. Above all, you need a powerful message that will move the reader to action.

Should we ask for a specific amount?

If possible, yes, but this is difficult if you do not know what the recipient of your letter can afford. But if you give no guidance you may get £5 from someone who could have given you much more.

One approach is to give check boxes for a range of donations on the reply card: say £10, £25, £100, £250 and 'other amounts', or a monthly standing order for £2.50, £5, £10 or £25. Be careful of putting amounts that are too small. Perhaps you could say that if the recipient cannot consider a substantial donation of the kind requested, they might help in another way, as a volunteer or by suggesting further names for your mailing list, or by writing in protest to the villain in your case.

By the way, an excellent American fundraising book refers to evidence that people most often choose the second if they are given four choices of amounts to give!

Tone and style

For many years, I have kept the following example of a commercial direct mail consultant's circular letter – nothing to do with charity – showing a highly successful professional's approach to a completely cold mailing. When reading other people's draft charity fundraising letters, I try to imagine his comments on them. You might also like to compare this with the style of the trust application letter on page 70.

Oh no!

NOT <u>ANOTHER</u> SALES LETTER

I suppose that as we are all expected to be Honest, Truthful and Legal these days, I had better come clean. The only excuse for this mailing is that every time I write a letter like this, business goes up by 25%.

Sounds too good to be true? Well, it must be added that it has taken 20 years of experience and about the same amount of time learning how to target mailings and to source lists.

I remember many years ago a pioneer of direct mail, long since gone to join the celestial postmaster in the sky, used to say to me: 'Keep it simple Mike – a brochure tells but a sales letter <u>SELLS!</u>' And he was absolutely right. Good direct mail can be amazingly simple, remarkably inexpensive and wonderfully effective. One of our clients <u>regularly</u> sells £1 million of his products using a two-colour sales letter we produced for him. The same letter ... over and over again ... <u>to the same lists</u>. Nothing is cheaper to produce, or harder working, than a good sales letter. After all, you are still reading this, aren't you?

Whatever the right approach may be – and if you need an all-singing and dancing, pop-up dayglo crashpack we can produce that too – we can create your mailing piece, supply the mailing list and mail it far cheaper and more effectively than you can do it yourself. <u>That's a promise</u>. In any area and any quantity and within the slimmest budgets.

Now that you are planning your autumn and Christmas campaigns, why not call me for some free advice on direct mail, design, copy and lists? Do it now and discover how to make direct mail work for you.

Michael Barford

Mike Barford

P.S. Act now and we'll show you how a silly PS like this can double your response!'

What should we do with the responses?

One of the most frequent complaints from the public is about the way we respond to the donations that we receive. Please ensure that within 48 hours you can, by post, phone or e-mail

- acknowledge receipt of the gift
- thank the donor
- cash the cheque (often forgotten, even when we have made a great fuss about how desperately the money is needed!).

You should also keep a record of when and how the above were done. I like to keep a photocopy of cheques on file; they can be surprisingly informative.

How do we measure the success of our mailings?

You should record

- the percentage response
- the most frequent size of gift (the 'mode', more useful than the average)
- the percentage cost (money spent/money received, times 100)
- comments, while they are still fresh in your mind.

Little reports like this make good items for trustees meetings, especially when they can be compared with previous mailings.

How often should we write?

The ideal answer is 'as often as the donor is happy to hear from you' – donors generally like hearing from the charities they support. If you acknowledge substantial donations with a thank-you telephone call (as well as the still obligatory immediate thank-you letter) this is an excellent opportunity to ask how often they are happy for you to write.

Otherwise the answer is usually 'more often than you would suppose'.

How long should I keep people on our mailing list if nothing appears?

As long as it is productive to do so. This is where it is enormously helpful to have good records and someone who is able to analyse them. What percentage response do you need to have to justify keeping names on the list? When it drops below that level, consider removing the names.

Where lists are of hundreds rather than thousands, I am against any automatic rules for deciding who to keep on and who to take off. You should be able to review each name individually – at the Directory of Social Change I found that this was perfectly possible even for a list of 10,000, but then I had lived with the list virtually from its creation.

For example, Mrs Brown may have been a big donor in the past, so why not give her a ring and ask her if she is still interested? Mr Jones may have given one modest donation because he was asked personally by one of your former trustees at a council reception, but has shown no interest since – OK, off he goes.

Even in quite large charities, there can probably be a list of only hundreds of major donors who between them account for a large proportion of the income, and they can be treated individually even if all the others get automatically removed from the list after, say, four no-response mailings.

Isn't all this sounding a bit technical?

Yes, it is. Direct mail is one of the most technical forms of fundraising (because of this it is often all too attractive to those of us who are scared of making direct person-to-person requests, for which it is usually no substitute). There is a whole industry around the creation of direct mail packs, the measurement and testing of responses and the planning of mailing schedules, with commercial agencies whose sole business this is.

I think that I have learnt three key lessons over the years:

- Results depend on the quality of your list, not its size.
- Testing is of key importance; even the experts cannot tell in advance which letter will work and which will not.
- A genuinely moving personal letter can break all the rules! I remember one in which a lady was too embarrassed even to ask for money. She just wrote along the lines of 'It is all so terrible that I just feel I must tell everybody I can what is going on', and the money rolled in. But I don't recommend this approach.

Many modest-sized charities have a great advantage in that they can make their mailings much more personal than those from a professional fundraising department of, say, 30 staff.

How should we respond to enquirers?

Promptly, politely and personally will be enough to put you well ahead in the game, almost regardless of the actual content of your reply (though it should include a response form for those who would like to give a donation). In 2003 professional fundraiser Ken Burnett sent out 50 enquiries to the largest charities from a fictitious would-be donor, Emma Cole, asking for information. Less than half replied within a week, 10 never answered at all and very few managed a personal reply. So you don't have to have any special magic; just be competent!

How should we respond to donations?

Promptly, personally and warmly. Another fundraising consultancy sent cheques for £15 each to 75 top charities, also in 2003. Nineteen of them sent no acknowledgement or thank you of any kind! Three hadn't even cashed the cheque within 12 weeks. Of those who did reply, some sent an impersonal and 'formulaic' letter of thanks that was 'little better than no thanks at all'.

How big do you really have to be before it becomes impractical for all your supporters to get a personally addressed and signed note from your chair or one of your trustees? And if you are genuinely too big for this, why not from a senior staff member – after all, the donors are paying their salaries.

What about mailings to our existing supporters?

These are a bit different to 'cold mailings'. Your aims are:

- to keep them giving, often by asking them to convert from occasional one-off donations to regular ongoing support. I would prefer to have a standing order for £25 a year than a single gift of £100;
- to encourage them to give more. This is often done by having special one-off appeals: 'Can you contribute to the rebuilding and expansion of our training centre?'

Can you ask for more money over and over again?

Well, yes, you can. After all, churches do it, every week, so it must be alright! It is easy to worry about sounding as if all you are after is the donors' money. Usually it is what you are after, and that is fine – though it is nice if you can also offer the option of becoming an active volunteer. The deal is that you have the ability to get something done that both of you think valuable, and the donors have the ability to give money towards it. This makes you partners in the same rewarding enterprise.

Approach donors with an offer to enable them to join in something really worthwhile and satisfying and they will respond happily. The partnership is real. Without the donors, nothing would happen. So it is important to constantly recognise the partnership as such, in all your letters and literature. If a life has been saved, a family helped, a musician trained or a woodland preserved, they have done this just as much as you have. Donors are not external to your work; they are an integral part of it.

Therefore one purpose of your mailings is to keep your partners up to date with how you are doing, but you can also ask again for money at the same time. Just do it nicely – for example you can enclose a gift envelope with the suggestion that, if they are already doing all they can for you themselves, they might know of someone else who would like to join in the work.

(In this context, few things are as unattractive as a few charities which have given the impression that their donors are simply milch cows whose role is to pay for professional staff to practise their own expert trade – one which the donors would be too simple-minded to understand.)

Door-to-door and public collections

House-to-house collections are an effective way of raising money if you have access to a suitable pool of committed volunteers happy to undertake it. But this is a big 'if'.

Do we need permission to go house to house?

Yes, you need to get a permit from your local authority, though if yours is a national collection you can get it authorised by the Charity Commission. The rules may change, so get detailed information from the Commission (www.charity-commission.gov.uk).

How do we organise the collection?

Conventionally, an envelope with an accompanying letter or brochure is dropped through the door. The collector then returns a few days later to collect the envelopes.

Your collectors need to be very well briefed and debriefed – the after-collecting gathering can also be a good little party in its own right. This is important because volunteers greatly value the social rewards they get from taking part in your collection. After all, there are very many other excellent causes they could do it for. They will tend to stick with the one that gives the most satisfying experience. It is not usually enough just to rely on commitment to your cause.

There are all sorts of variations. See the following box about the Karuna Trust.

The Karuna Trust

Many years ago two people from the Karuna Trust came on one of our training courses; I was embarrassed as they knew far more about the realities of face-to-face fundraising than I did. The charity raises money in Britain for Buddhist welfare and educational projects in India. Done mainly house to house by young volunteers, I regard a successful spell with Karuna as one of the best qualifications a fundraiser can have.

Manjuka describes the operation as follows, though he does not mention that the fundraisers are backed up by some of the finest and most moving charity literature that I have ever seen, especially in its use of photographs (to be inspired, send an appropriate donation and get a copy of the latest annual report: details on www.karuna.org).

The Karuna Trust works in India amongst Dalit communities doing education, skills training, health and cultural projects. Karuna has been fundraising door to door soliciting Gift Aid Standing Orders for over twenty years. There are currently over 8,000 regular donors recruited in this way, providing a reliable income stream for the charity. These donors account for some 90% of an annual income of just over £1 million.

Karuna runs seven appeals annually, each lasting about six weeks with teams of up to seven fundraisers. Each appeal is in a different city, which is scouted ahead to find suitable areas – finding good areas is a bit of an art form, but the basic principle is that the exterior of a house says a lot about who lives inside. Obviously some people are more likely to sign up than others and therefore some houses are more likely to be worth knocking than others. The teams live together in a rented house and are guided through the experience by a leader from Karuna.

Our fundraisers are largely volunteers. As Karuna was set up and is run by Buddhists the volunteers are recruited from the Buddhist community so they tend to be self-aware, positive and communicative types, although they need not be extroverted – all temperaments can fundraise, what matters is their positive motivation. Ages have ranged from 20 to 74. Fundraising like this is an exhilarating experience. You never know what is going to happen next, who you are going to meet, how they will respond. It very much places you in the moment. If the fundraiser can embrace this experience with its attendant fears and uncertainties then they will be vibrant and interesting to the householders answering the door.

We just try and meet people and communicate with them. If a person is busy when we meet them on a door we notice and acknowledge that. The aim of the initial visit is to leave an introductory booklet that will allow the potential donor to consider whether Karuna is something they would like to support. The fundraiser then returns a few days later, once the potential donor has had a chance to think it through. Taking genuine interest and showing sensitivity and respect to householders is something most appreciate and benefit from. This creates a space into which they may become interested in Karuna.

To this end our fundraisers are trained in the art of communication. A range of training methods are used including role play, story telling, games, body workshops, meditation. Approached in this way, householders are seldom rude or abusive to the fundraisers. Our approach results in many happy donors who invariably thank us for giving them the opportunity to give. We are so successful because we are like the bee that takes the pollen from the flower, leaving it unharmed with renewed potential to grow and develop.

What about street collections...

These are more difficult than house-to-house ones and seem to be declining. You will need a local authority permit, numerous volunteers for what is often seen as a rather unattractive chore and sealed collection devices. These last are available from commercial suppliers pre-printed with your logo and so on. For contact details, see www.fundraising.co.uk.

It is essential to have a proper system for collecting, counting and recording the money (for instance you must have at least two people there when the boxes are opened and the money counted and recorded).

It may be easier to have your collections in public places that are not streets, like shopping centres, where you just need the permission of the owners; but they may be reluctant to give this.

... and about face-to-face fundraising in the street?

This is rapidly developing, highly successful and very controversial. It normally involves young people, employed by professional fundraising agencies, approaching members of the public in the street and asking them to commit to regular monthly donations by standing order or direct debit.

A few people complain vociferously about being harassed by relays of such people as they walk down the street (though this has never happened to me, despite working most of my time in central London – perhaps I look too broke).

It is highly expensive to get started, with most of the first year's donations usually going to the collecting agency, but as it brings in a high proportion of long-term supporters this is well worth it.

The practice is developing in different ways. A few charities are seeking to train volunteers to do this kind of collecting – though an exceptionally high degree of commitment would seem to be needed. Others are trying to reduce the bluntness of approaching just anybody. The NSPCC, for example, is asking for money in the context of a display about the work of the charity, and concentrating on people who indicate some degree of interest by approaching the stand.

It is, so far, confined to fairly large charities, especially those thought to be attractive to the relatively youthful donor – it was pioneered in Britain by Greenpeace – but this may be changing. Rethink, the former National Schizophrenia Fellowship, is reporting excellent results for a very different kind of charity. The initial investment is nevertheless too high for many smaller charities.

Can it be right to approach complete strangers in the street?

In my view, it is absolutely alright, and I see this development as an excellent thing. Just as the main reason that people donate to charity is that they are asked, so too the main reason they do not give is that they are not asked.

When I ask people in large meetings to put up their hands if they have been personally and directly asked to make a serious donation or commitment to a charity in the last twelve months, I expect a response of less than six per cent. When I then ask 'haven't you forgotten about your church?' I get a few more (many people don't think of their church or temple or whatever as a charity, but it is). But even so, most people are simply never asked personally for a substantial donation (as opposed to the fiver into a tin).

Not many years ago, almost everyone went to church or some other religious place, and so almost everyone was regularly asked to donate, not just to the church but often to a whole range of associated charities. We badly need something to replace this systematic asking and so I welcome the new in-the-street 'direct dialogue' fundraising, as it is called.

As for being harassed, am I too harsh in having limited time for those who, in response to a polite charitable appeal, can't manage an equally polite 'No, thank you'?

Direct requests for donations

Just asking people for money, face to face or on the phone, has the highest response rate of any form of fundraising. It is also quite threatening for many potential 'askers', who are embarrassed by the thought of talking to people about money – this is one reason why people are so tempted by any other form of fundraising that will avoid this situation.

It is essential to recognise that you are not asking for money for your own benefit, but for the children, or the ballet, or whatever. You also need to remember that the donor gets a lot in return – satisfaction of a kind that is much valued. So you are not a beggar seeking alms, but you are more like a salesperson offering something that people want – usually a warm and perhaps even unaccustomed glow of virtue – in return for the money.

In another book, Michael Norton, the founder of the Directory of Social Change, quotes an example of the ideal approach, from Rtn G A Rao, the Treasurer of the Bangalore Hospice in India: 'I am utterly shameless, I have no hesitation in asking my friends and persons to whom I am introduced for donations to a cause I believe in. After all, I am not asking for myself'.

Won't I upset the people I ask?

This would be pretty unusual. You have complimented them by showing you believe them to be a generous person who might both like and be able to help a good cause.

How can I prepare for rejection or argument?

You could think about dealing with people's responses in the following ways:

- The person says 'sorry, no', with or without giving a reason. This will happen, as far as I can tell, about 50% of the time. It is quite OK for someone to say 'no' and they do not have to say why. You just thank them pleasantly for listening and move on (don't try to change their mind, at least, not on the spot). Remember, it is not you that is being rejected, but the proposition that you have put, and there are plenty more fish in the sea. Mostly the reason for the 'no' will be nothing to do with you or your charity anyway; it may be the letter from the bank that morning, the fact that the soup is about to boil over or because they are waiting for another call on the phone. Or they may genuinely be already wholly committed to supporting other charities.
- She or he asks questions you can't answer. Get fully briefed, if you are not already. Just go through with colleagues all the most likely questions. Then, if you get one that you did not expect, you can just say so, explaining what you do and do not know.

How can I get into this gently?

An excellent half-way house is to start with groups rather than individuals. For example, ask if you can come and talk to church groups, Women's Institutes and so on to explain what you are doing and ask for support. If you do this, it is always a great help to have pictures to show people, either by handing them round or using a projector (but the story still needs to be told).

The most successful appeal I ever saw was by a very young woman from a playgroup for disabled children in York. I had arranged for her to speak to about 80 engineering workers in a factory at their weekly staff training session. She said where she was from, 'the place down the road outside and on the left', and that unless they got some more money the playgroup would close and the children would have nowhere to go. She then burst into tears and ran out of the room, whereupon I collected 60 or so signatures for substantial donations.

Some people use videos so that they do not have to make the request themselves. Personally, I dislike most video appeals as they break the person-to-person contact.

Does it become easy after a time?

For most of us, perhaps, it becomes much less difficult with experience (indeed after just the first one or two times), but no, it will probably never become easy. However the kick when people agree to support your cause is terrific and more than enough reward even if it stays hard to do. It is so astonishingly productive and rewarding that this quickly comes to outweigh the nervousness we continue to feel. And you will enjoy the admiration and respect of all around!

There are indeed people who simply don't have any problem asking for money for a good cause, and they are worth their weight in gold. Getting them to support your charity, because you are such fun to work with, will probably be one of your aims.

Major gifts

This is where most fundraising began and is it is still a core fundraising component for many charities, especially those with access to a middle-class constituency.

In 1990 I was in Hungary and saw the overpainting being stripped from the old sign in a special school on which the names of the original patrons and subscribers in the 1930s had been inscribed. It was a visible reappearance of the old notion of philanthropy after nearly 50 years of communism – the notion that those who are doing well should give money to help those who are less fortunate. This idea is still widely accepted by the prosperous, as indeed it should be. But they do usually need to be asked.

For many of us, the problem is that society has become so physically segregated that there may be very few well-off people anywhere near where you are working. In such cases consider going to where the money is. I have sat in a Hackney room listening to tales about everyone on the estate being unemployed or on a very low income, even while the setting sun passed behind the tower buildings of the great banks in the City of London just up the road. When the group shifted its efforts up there, they were able to prosper.

How do you bridge the gap between rich and poor, if this is what you want to do? There is no single way, but I have found that few groups are wholly without contacts to the better off. Churches are often a good meeting ground. In almost every area there are people with reputations for generosity and often with excellent contacts. Do not forget that such people are looking for you, in a general way, as well as you looking for them. They know that they have had all the breaks and are often seeking opportunities to share their good fortune with others who have not been so lucky.

What is a major gift?

For a small, wholly voluntary organisation it might be as little as £250. For a nationally known 'brand name' charity it might be as much as £10,000.

They are often sought as part of a capital appeal (see page 57) but charities can also have a group of key regular supporters, perhaps called patrons or some other such title. In Oxford University they get recognition through, among other things, a public procession in spectacular academic gowns designed for the purpose.

In either case such gifts will usually come because the donor has been identified and personally asked for the gift by a trustee or a pretty senior member of staff – seldom by professional fundraising staff.

How do we seek such donors?

First, you work hard to make a list of possible major donors. They may come from among your existing supporters, they could be people already known for their generosity in your area or field of work, or they could just be identified by determined networking, usually by your trustees: 'I will ask Mrs Hudson; she knows every likely donor round here' and so on.

Second, you farm out the work of asking them, so that you have a list of who is to be asked by whom. This can be left to the askers to get on with in their own way (though they will need a lot of chasing, which should be your chair's job in many cases) or you can organise a social event which will give a good opportunity to ask at least some of them.

4 Events and fundraising activities

I have not headed this 'fundraising events' because many charity events meet more than one aim. Indeed the main aim may be to publicise your activities, with fundraising a secondary consideration. You have already seen an example in the box about the Brent River Society on page 35.

Apart from that there are four main categories of event (though they can overlap):

- fundraising gatherings
- 'pay-to-come' events
- sponsored events
- lotteries and games.

Can you raise money from social events?

An absolutely routine approach in American fundraising, these events are for some reason less frequent in Britain – a pity as they are a straightforward way to raise money. You ask potential donors for a drink or a meal in your or another supporter's home – anything from a coffee morning to a barbecue – at which you explain what your charity is doing and ask for donations. People like to come as it will be a pleasant social occasion in a good cause.

Those invited need to be confident that they will not be pressed to give more than they can manage without pain. As invitations will generally be face to face or by phone, you can easily reassure people about this. One approach is to say that if they can't contribute significant money themselves, they are still welcome to come and help in some other way – by finding out about what they can do as volunteers, or by contributing suggestions of other people whom you might approach, or indeed just by helping run the event.

At the event, though, it is important to actually ask people to contribute – they are, of course, expecting this. However it may be sensible to ensure in advance that the first person you ask will respond positively and generously.

There are many ways of organising such get-togethers. One spectacularly large-scale example is Macmillan Cancer Relief's 'World's Biggest Coffee Morning' (www.macmillan.org.uk).

Extract from a Plymouth newspaper, 2003

Fundraising socially

ST JUDE'S salon owner Julie Hutton has raised a staggering £7,386 for St Luke's Hospice. Mrs Hutton gathered friends and family at her home for a strawberries and champagne silver service party. The event was in memory of her mum, who died at the beginning of this year. The afternoon's biggest donation came from the sale of a huge year 2000 bottle of salmanazar Champagne, which was auctioned for £400.

'Pay-to-come' or 'pay-to-take-part' fundraising events

These again cover a huge range from the car boot sale on the school playground to the classical music recital with champagne supper in the country house.

Most local fundraising events, if they are to be cost effective, need to be organised and managed by volunteers. Only larger, high-price ticket affairs justify hands-on management by professional fundraisers.

The big charities have what are called 'community fundraisers', a main part of whose job is to travel their area encouraging local volunteers to organise such events. Even so, neither the amounts raised, nor the cost of raising them, tend to be very attractive in themselves. The hope is more that they will attract new supporters who can be 'converted' into regular donors, especially those able to give bigger gifts or to write the charity into their wills. However community fundraising seems to be declining in importance for these big charities, who find the returns too low for the substantial costs involved. In 2003 a Red Cross fundraising manager suggested that charities should drop community fundraising activities that failed to return at least £2 for every £1 invested, rightly implying that many failed to reach this target.

On the other hand, charities with committed volunteers can often leave them to get on with it on their own, with only a limited investment of money or of the time of professional staff. Even here, though, it is easy for your trustees to put their scarce time into these often quite unrewarding activities, when they should be focusing on more productive ways of bringing in the money that is needed.

The costs of events and lotteries

Events and lotteries can be a successful and important part of a charity's fundraising, occasionally the main or even the only part. However, too often they are organised in place of the generally more effective straight pursuit of individual donations.

They are usually a costly way of raising money and first appearances may deceive. A recent detailed study found that 'events are one of the least productive methods for a charity to generate income'. Do your sums carefully.

As an example, look at the following gross income figures, from a recent set of accounts from the excellent National Blind Children's Society:

Lotteries and games	£427,000
Donations and legacies	£422,000
Fundraising events	£315,000

From this, you might suppose that the lotteries and games were the biggest of the three sources of income. But if you look at the net income remaining to be used for the work of the charity, after taking away the relevant fundraising costs, the picture is quite different:

Donations and legacies	£361,000 (after fundraising costs of £61,000)
Lotteries and games	£184,000 (after fundraising costs of £198,000)
Fundraising events	£138,000 (after fundraising costs of £164,000)

Note however, that there is nothing wrong with activities such as events or lotteries having a high level of expenses, if these are incurred in providing prizes, parties or other benefits to the participants. The people who take part are paying for these benefits as well as making a donation to your charity. And if you do not offer good value, they will stop coming.

What about sponsored events?

I expect all of you have come across such events – 'Will you sponsor me for a three-hour silence?', or 'a marathon?', or a thousand other things. A more recent development is the sponsorship of individuals for what can appear to be little more than adventure holidays – climbing Mount Kilimanjaro or whatever. In some cases this has developed into something very near 'trading', with the charity, usually through a trading subsidiary, becoming a holiday organiser and taking the profits (though the holidays are actually often organised for the charity by a professional travel company).

Among big national charities, reliance on sponsored events, often elaborate, has been growing in recent years though there is a feeling that the boom may now have peaked – if only because a whole lot of new charities are coming into the field having seen the success of the pioneers (and perhaps not realising that success is harder than it looks).

What are 'subsidiary trading companies'?

All charities can trade as part of their charitable activities – the Directory of Social Change, publisher of this book and itself a charity, earns money from its publishing. As educating and informing people who work for charities is within its charitable purposes, this is no problem. But DSC could not earn money by selling its books to help commercial businesses manage themselves better; this would be trading outside its charitable purposes.

If DSC thought it could earn substantial money from such non-charitable publishing to support its charitable activities, it would have to set up a trading subsidiary to do so. This subsidiary company would then donate all its profits to DSC.

The field is complicated and professional advice is needed at an early stage. The situation is set out in full in the *Voluntary Sector Legal Handbook*, also published by DSC.

Caution!

Some events carry big financial risks. Be very careful not to get into something that you cannot afford to see go wrong. It may pour with rain, or the celebrity entertainer may cry off, leaving you with all the fixed costs of the marquee, sound system and catering contract, or whatever. If it can happen, it will, sooner or later, and the possibility must have been allowed for.

The Brent River Park barbecue

This was one of the first fundraising events with which I was involved. There is, in Hanwell, west London, a thatched cottage with a wood, a pond and a stream. The owner, herself on our committee, let us use this lovely and private place for a midsummer barbecue. Almost everything was provided free: tents and portable loos from the scouts, sound systems and DJs from local enthusiasts, tables and chairs from the church hall, square dance calling from the council water cleanliness officer who we knew otherwise in his professional capacity, and so on. Tickets were sold in advance, providing the cash with which to buy the food and drink.

The event ran successfully for years, with its own committee and little other input from the charity, and provided a good proportion of our annual income.

Managing an events programme

A key principle here is replicability. Successful events are usually a lot of work to set up the first time, but once established can usually be repeated annually (or more often) far more easily. Everyone knows what has to be done and they can just get on with it (though as people change and move, it is very much safer if a fairly detailed note of all the arrangements exists, even if only in the background).

The ideal is a 'portfolio' of repeated fundraising events. For example, say six events annually, with one new one being introduced and the least successful of the old ones being dropped.

Ideas for events are almost unlimited – just ask everyone to keep their eyes and ears open for what other people are doing and pick out the ones that attract you and your colleagues. An element of your own originality and imagination is very helpful, but it is unwise to risk much time or money on a totally new concept.

An attraction of events is that you can raise money for almost any cause in this way. People did not come to the Brent River Society barbecue so much because of their deep environmental commitment as because it was an excellent and unusual party. Years ago, I came across a very successful celebrity cricket match organised by a charity with a completely 'anonymous' name, like the Axis Trust. I had to look it up in the Charity Commission to find out that it was in fact one of the early HIV/AIDS appeals, at a time when there was a pretty strong stigma attached to the HIV issue. It didn't matter, as people were there for the cricket and the socialising and just had a vague understanding that it was all in a good cause.

Lotteries and games

These are not an easy alternative to conventional fundraising, but they can be effective if well managed. For example, see the example of the National Blind Children's Society on page 53 above, who sold £427,000-worth of lottery tickets at a cost in prizes and other administrative charges of £198,000, leaving them with a surplus of £184,000. The charity noted in its annual report that 53% is the average proportion of income that is needed for prizes and administration, according to the Lottery Council.

There are all sorts of regulations surrounding lotteries that you need to be aware of, set out in a leaflet from the Gaming Board 'Lotteries and the Law' (www.gbgb.org.uk has the text).

5 Capital appeals

What is a capital appeal?

This is usually a one-off campaign to raise money for a specific development, often a building, but it might also relate to a new programme or project. It is separate and additional to ongoing fundraising for the charity's day-to-day running costs.

Organising an appeal

Unlike most other forms of fundraising, there is a fairly well-established routine from which it would be risky to deviate too far. There are a number of stages:

- **Planning**. You will usually need a detailed plan for the work and its funding arrangements, often including a business plan or feasibility study. If you have limited experience of such a task, at the very least talk to people who have organised similar projects elsewhere.

- **Establishing an appeal committee**. These are committees of volunteers willing and able to ask for significant sums of money. Leadership is key. The chair needs to be someone who will commit themselves to the appeal's success (not just a big name figurehead) and he or she will probably have previous experience of such appeals. You could try asking around to find who have been active and successful members of earlier appeal committees in your area or field of work – perhaps the time has come for them to lead their own.

- **Setting your targets**. It is usual to break down the donations required by number and size and then to write down the prospective donors for each band – assuming, perhaps, that you will need four prospects for each gift of a particular size, but allowing for another of the four to give a lesser gift. Suppose your new building will cost £1 million and you have been offered half of this amount from one of the Lottery funds, but must raise the other £500,000 yourselves. The table might look like this:

Amount	No. of gifts	Total
£100,000	1 donation	£100,000
£20,000 to £50,000	4 donations	£120,000
£10,000 to £20,000	10 donations	£130,000
£1,000 to £10,000	20 donations	£100,000
Less than £1,000	200 donations	£ 50,000
Total		£500,000

The plan may include some grants from trusts and foundations, or from other public sources, as well as from individuals.

- **Agreeing a programme of work.** Who will ask these people for their donations, where and how? There is probably a range of events to be organised, from private lunches to a public launch.

- **Implementation.** A substantial proportion of the large donations needs to be secured 'in principle' before the campaign is publicly launched. This will give confidence to donors that they are associating themselves with something that is clearly going to succeed. If you cannot put the lead donations together in private discussions, you may have to rethink the whole appeal.

Using fundraising consultants

This is a field in which it may be worth talking to consultants, many of whom specialise in such appeals (NCVO has a list of fundraising consultants). They will normally come and talk to you free of charge in advance of any commitment and will probably be able to give you a useful and early view on whether or not your plans are realistic. You will still be under no obligation to make any further use of their services.

6 Raising money from trusts and foundations

What are trusts and foundations?

These are charities that give money in grants to other charities. But note that their name may not include either of these words, 'trust' or 'foundation' – BBC Children in Need, for example – and note also that very many organisations with the word 'trust' or 'foundation' in their name do not make grants – the Terrence Higgins Trust, for example, is a fundraising charity like yours. You know them by what they do, not by what they are called.

How do you get grants from them?

You write and ask for a grant (a few have application forms), enclosing a copy of your annual report and accounts. They write back saying 'Yes' or 'No'. On average, about one in every four such letters results in a grant (though not necessarily for the full amount requested).

For many charities this is the easiest, cheapest form of fundraising but note two important cautions.

Two cautions!

1   Trust grants on their own will seldom produce enough income for any but the smallest, wholly voluntary, charities.

2   This is usually short-term money and cannot be relied on as regular support for the delivery of ongoing services or activities.

Researching a particular trust

Grantmaking trusts come in a huge range of shapes and sizes. Here are some of the ways one can differ from another.

Is the trust general or specialised?

- The Tanner Trust (annual grant total about £175,000) gives grants, mostly of less than £1,000, to many kinds of charity, local, national and international.

- The Cooks Charity (£100,000 a year) supports education in catering and in one year gave just four grants of £25,000 each.

Is the trust big or small?

The biggest grantmakers listed in 2003 were:

Wellcome Trust	£388 million	Biomedical research
The Sainsbury family trusts	£56 million	A range of very specific fields of interest
Garfield Weston Foundation	£33 million	General, in the UK
PPP Foundation	£26 million	Healthcare research and development
Esmée Fairbairn Foundation	£26 million	Welfare, education, environment, arts and heritage
BBC Children in Need	£25 million	Welfare of disadvantaged children

On the other hand there are thousands which give away less than £5,000 a year.

Does the trust make big grants or small grants?

Not quite the same thing. The Parthenon Trust (£12 million in the year) gives few grants of less than £50,000. The even larger Lloyds TSB Foundations (£27 million) give few that are for as much as that.

Does the trust have an office and professional staff?

The mighty Sainsbury family trusts maintain a large and expert staff. The similarly sized Garfield Weston Foundation has very few. Most trusts have no staff at all and your letters are opened and dealt with by the trustees – all volunteers – and usually in their own homes.

When the grant total rises above a hundred thousand pounds or so, many trustees begin to employ either a part-time administrator or they ask their solicitors or accountants to handle the correspondence and the making of payments, while the trustees still do the decision making. Much bigger than this and you begin to see professional grantmaking staff who investigate applications and advise trustees accordingly.

Does the trust have clear policies and guidelines?

Some trusts are clear and specific about what they will fund. Others say something like 'all applications will be considered on their merits', or say nothing at all – though they may well offer a list of what they will not fund. For example, funding from the Sherburn House Charity, in the Durham area, is to 'relieve need, hardship and distress' and it notes areas of interest such as disability or community needs, but it also has a list of 15 'exclusions' such as 'organisations that are in serious deficit' or 'hospitals and medical centres (except hospices)'.

An example of 'guidelines'

Phrases such as 'guidelines for applicants' can mean almost anything. Many trusts have none at all, or they are simply lists of what information is called for and how it is to be submitted, without indicating the policies of the trust at all. The following guidelines, from the MacRobert Trust in Scotland, fall somewhere in the middle. It gives away over £500,000 a year, mostly to Scottish charities. (NB Their affection for capital letters is often found amongst trusts.)

Advice to applicants

Lady MacRobert recognised that new occasions teach new duties and therefore the new Trust deed gives wide discretionary powers to the Trustees. The Trust is reactive so, with very few exceptions, grants are made only in response to applications made through the correct channels.

The Trustees reconsider their policy and practice of grant giving every five years. The beneficial area is United Kingdom-wide but preference is given to organisations in Scotland. Grants are normally made only to a recognised Scottish Charity or a recognised charity outside Scotland.

Trust's categories of interest
Currently, the major categories under which the Trustees consider support are:

- Science and Technology
- Youth
- Services and Sea
- Disabled and Handicapped
- Ex-Servicemen's Hospital and Homes

- Education
- Community Welfare

The Minor Categories are:

- Agriculture and Horticulture
- Arts and Music
- Medical Care
- Tarland and Deeside

The Trustees look for clear, realistic and attainable aims. Grants vary but most lie between £5,000 and £10,000. Occasionally the Trustees make a recurring grant of up to three years.

The Trustees recognise the need to assist voluntary organisations which need funds to complement those already received from central government and local authority sources. However, this is not to say that the Trust makes a grant where statutory bodies fail to provide.

The Trustees are prepared to make core/revenue grants where appropriate but favour projects.

The Trustees recognise that, at present, experiment and innovation are much more difficult to fund and the Trust's role in funding them the more significant.

What the trust does not support
As a broad guide, grants are not normally provided for:

- Religious organisations (but not including youth/community services provided by them, or projects of general benefit to the whole community)
- Organisations based outside the United Kingdom
- Individuals
- Endowment or memorial funds
- General appeals or mailshots
- Political organisations
- Student bodies as opposed to universities
- Fee-paying schools, apart from an Educational Grants Scheme for children who are at, or who need to attend, a Scottish independent secondary school and for which a grant application is made through the Head Teacher
- Expeditions
- Retrospective grants

- Departments within a university, unless the appeal gains the support of, and is channelled through, the principal

Time-bars

- Unsuccessful applicants must pause for at least one year from the time of being notified before reapplying
- Successful applicants must pause for at least two years from the time of receiving a grant before reapplying. In the case of a two or three-year recurring grant the time-bar applies from the time of receiving the last instalment.

Where does the trust get its money?

Some trusts are 'endowed', that is they give away the income generated by their permanent and invested capital endowment which was the original donation by their founder – often through his or her will.

Sometimes the founder or founders may still be alive, in which case they may act more like a single wealthy donor rather than an institution of any kind. The huge new Rausing foundations are much like this.

Other foundations earn or collect their money as they go along, like Comic Relief or the declining Foundation for Sport and the Arts which is funded annually from the profits of the football pools companies. These tend to be more formal in their grantmaking, as they are answerable to those who put up the money.

How long does it take to get a decision?

Seldom less than two months, often up to six months or even a year. Trusts are not a source of fast emergency funding (unless they already know you well and will treat you as an exception).

Trust grantmaking

What do trusts like to fund?

It can be almost anything; just a straight donation to charities whose letters they like; a development or research activity, or a 'capital' project like building works. Many appear to be 'policy free' – meaning that all applications will be considered on their merits, and they will not say what 'merit' consists of. Others are quite specific, either because of the way they were set up – the City Parochial Foundation is for the benefit of the poor of London – or because of the sometimes very specific decisions of the present trustees – one of the many Sainsbury family trusts, for example, is concerned at present with the environmental effects of aviation, among other things.

What do trusts not like to fund?

Most often, and for good reason, trusts generally are reluctant to fund the ongoing costs of what you do. This is not their fault, but is inherent in the idea of grantmaking in the first place. Their business is making funding decisions. In order to decide on new grants they must bring old ones to an end, otherwise they become silted up, just supporting the same charities every year and to that extent putting themselves out of the deciding business. But nevertheless a few have done exactly this, especially local trusts, and they support almost exactly the same charities year after year, while many others have at least a few 'old faithfuls' whom they support indefinitely.

Unfortunately, few trusts like helping charities that have got into difficulties. Supporting the already successful is generally found more attractive!

Do I have to be a skilled application writer?

I don't think so. You just need a good cause, presented in a way that you yourself would find convincing. Trusts rapidly become fairly good at extracting the gist of any application, and many quite dreadfully written applications result in grants. There is, though, a frequent distaste for the idea of professional trust fundraisers and if the application gives the impression of having come from such a source, this may count against it – trusts generally prefer to talk to the people who will be doing the work that they fund.

Trusts are regularly annoyed by applicants whose letters show that they have not even read the information available about what the funding body does.

Caution!

You may meet operational colleagues who say that fundraising is your business, not theirs. This is nonsense. It is fundraising that pays their salaries and supports their beneficiaries. And the price of being able to benefit others through an independent charity is raising the necessary money. If your colleagues don't like playing their part in this, perhaps they would be better off working for a statutory service.

Finding out about trusts

What information is available?

Many trusts produce some sort of 'guidelines for applicants', though even more do not. Where these exist, they must be read, but note that some trusts take their own guidelines more seriously than others, and most make at least some exceptions to their own policies.

Only a minority of trusts has informative annual reports (though they all should do so, just like other charities) but nearly all now have a grants list with their annual accounts. These lists enable their policies to be deduced, at least to some extent.

For an example of an excellent set of guidelines, see www.tudortrust.org.uk. For a bigger website with more comprehensive information, including the full annual report and grants lists, try www.johnlyonscharity.org.uk.

How do I find it?

1   Though not necessarily the best starting point, almost all the available information is printed in the grant guides published by the Directory of Social Change (DSC), the publishers also of this book, or is available electronically from the DSC's Trustfunding subscription website or CD-ROM . (You can find information about these products on www.dsc.org.uk and in 'Further reading' on page 83).

In many cases these books will also direct you to the trust's own website. The dedicated professional trust researcher (yes, there are indeed such people) may also use the Charity Commission register to look for any recent changes in trust addresses or trustees, or use the internet to research the background of individual trustees.

2   For many charities the full record of their dealings with trusts in the past, be they formal or informal, is particularly important as most trusts value a previous connection. Unfortunately, although the trusts usually have details accessibly filed about all your previous applications or grants, this is often not so the other way round. The lives of applicant charities are often turbulent, with record keeping being a low priority. It is worth trying to reconstruct such a history if it is not readily available – especially where informal personal contacts were established. These may be more important than any paperwork.

3   Another excellent starting point may be to find out, by asking, which trusts support other charities like yours.

From these sources it is usual to create a first list of your target trusts.

Which trusts should go on my 'target list'?

You need to find trusts that support your kind of work, or have a particular interest in your locality, or where you have or can develop a personal connection, and which have no 'exclusions' that apply to you – 'no grants for physical disability', or whatever.

You can go to the books directly and just start reading through them, use their indices, or use the search facilities on the CD-ROM or the trustfunding.org website. A word of caution, though, about these indices: they can only be partially successful because many trusts supply such limited information that the indexing is inevitably a bit hit or miss. For serious fundraising, there will often be no alternative to a careful individual assessment of each possible trust as far as your own charity is concerned. In no cases will the indices give you a mailing list that you can use without actually reading about each individual trust, especially its information on how to apply and on what is excluded.

If you do go straight to the books, one odd word of advice – do not start at A and work towards Z. We once found that of two very similar trusts, the one at the start of the alphabet was getting twice the number of applications as the one at the end. Presumably many people started at the beginning and never got to Z, I hope because they were already getting all the grants they could handle.

Applying for grants

Should I talk to the trusts first?

Yes, do this whenever it is sensible, but only after reading all their published guidelines (if these exist). To do otherwise greatly annoys (though your first call may simply be to ask for an up-to-date set of guidelines, or even to enquire if they have any).

Won't they just say 'send in your application'?

Some will, which is fine, but more and more trusts actively encourage such calls – after all, they may be able to dissuade you from sending in a hopeless application which would waste their time as well as yours. But with others, they may have a published dislike of preliminary phone calls, there may be no published phone number, or the number may be that of a purely administrative intermediary, like a firm of accountants, which actually plays no part in deciding on the grants. And beware, you may think you are ringing an office, but it may well be a voluntary trustee on her or his home number for whom the trust's affairs are just a very small part of a busy life.

What kind of calls do trusts like?

By and large they welcome sensible calls and much dislike time-wasting ones – of which they say they get quite a few.

What is a sensible call?

It will vary according to the information available, but it could be something like one of the following (depending on the published information available).

- 'I have read your guidelines and we have two kinds of work that we can ask you to support. Can you tell me which of them your trust is more likely to find interesting?'
- 'I can send you a full 36-page proposal complete with business plan, or would you just prefer a simple letter at this stage?'
- 'When do I need to get you my application for it to go the next trustees' meeting?'

What is the kind of call that annoys them?

Asking a question to which the answer is already published in their guidelines, on their website or in the trust directories.

How many applications should we send in?

Up to you, but the more you ask, the more you are likely to get. If your chances of success are one in four, then to approach only three trusts means you are most likely to receive nothing.

Do the trusts have application forms?

Rarely. Of the 30 biggest, only 10 have application forms and this becomes even less usual among smaller trusts. Most just ask for a letter, with appropriate attachments such as your annual report and accounts.

Sometimes there is a form to make sure you give the basic information, which has to be backed up by explanation of what you are asking them to support. Personally I dislike forms, as I am more comfortable being able to put my case in my own way. However I seem to be in a minority and it looks as if trusts with forms get more applications than those without, all else being equal.

Caution!

Many trustees do not want 'funding applications', just letters to themselves. They value the personal and tend to dislike the institutional. Wouldn't you, if, say, it was a family trust in memory of your grandad? I hear many complaints about inappropriate language: 'Who do they think we are – a local authority?'

What should I say in my letter?

If the trust spells out what it wants you to send, send it. Otherwise it depends on who you are writing to. This can vary from a trustee of a family trust who opens your letter at the breakfast table, through a harassed administrator handling many applications for small grants and with little time to spend on each, to experts in your field, looking for the best investments for their money.

If what you want to do is simple and self explanatory, does your community centre need to say any more than the following?

> Can your trust give us £10,000 so that we can continue our lunch clubs for over 30 isolated elderly people every day? The problem is that our ancient kitchen has been condemned – rightly – and it will cost this much to put it right. I attach details of the repairs that are needed, who we are and what we do.

How long can my letter be?

We have already covered some of the general points on letter writing on pages 37–39. Trusts are not much different, except that they are already committed to giving money away to some charity, even if not yours, and so get many letters. Though they are seldom 'swamped' by them as they often complain – even a large trust will be unusual if it gets more than eight applications in the working day – they do feel swamped and take every opportunity to ask applicants to make their letters shorter.

My experience is that shorter applications are also better in other respects, provided all the requested information is also attached.

I have never met an application so complicated that the request cannot be put across on a single, uncrowded page, although I am told that unfortunately few succeed in being as short as this. You can attach as much detail as you like, or as is called for, but in my experience decisions are far more often based on immediate reactions rather than on detailed study (though this immediate reaction may then be modified if the back-up material, such as your accounts, is absent or too weak).

I suggest that the single page might include the following.

• At the start, if possible, explain **why you are writing to them** (as opposed to sending a 'circular' letter to every trust you can think of): 'I am writing because five years ago you gave us a badly needed grant for ...'; or '... at the suggestion of your grateful grantholders at xyz charity'; or '... because your trust is an important supporter of work for the rights of ...'; or '... at the suggestion of Mrs ..., whom I believe you know' or '... following our brief conversation on the phone yesterday'. Even a minimal thing like this means your letter is unlikely to be seen as a 'circular'.

• Also at the beginning, in just one sentence, say **what you want**: 'Will you give us £x for y?' (Otherwise they will just start skipping to the end to see what you are asking for.)

• Say **what the problem is** that a grant from them will address – this should normally be your beneficiaries' problem, rather than your organisation's problem. For example, 'with £10,000 we can ensure the future of lunch clubs for hundreds of isolated elderly people every year ' rather than 'with £10,000 we can rebuild our community centre's kitchen which has been condemned by the health and safety inspector'.

• Describe **what you will do** about the problem: 'With the £10,000 we will not only meet all the new regulations but we will do it in a way that enables the old people themselves to play a far larger part in preparing the meals – which they greatly enjoy'.

• Explain **how you arrived at the figure you are requesting**: 'I attach a copy of the costings; we have been able to get the price down to £9,000 from the original estimate of £16,000. I hope that you will agree that another £1,000 for contingency costs is also prudent'.

• **Repeat the request**: 'We do hope you can give us this grant. If you can, the elderly club members will be so relieved – for many, it is the main part of their entire social life'.

• **Note the attachments** you are enclosing.

What about tone, style and appearance?

• This is a personal letter, not a business letter. Neither you nor they are businesses and a business style is inappropriate and off-putting – especially for trustees who widely deplore what they see as an increase in fundraising professionalism at the expense of what they see as personal commitment. In my view, for most charities, the letters usually come best from your own trustees (provided the trustee is closely concerned with the work in question). If no trustee is sufficiently involved, then it should come from the most senior person closely concerned with the issue.

- You should avoid the appearance of the word-processed, mail-merged appeal – you know the sort of thing, perhaps: 'You will remember, Mrs J D Martin, ...'. Always try to find a named person to write to, rather than 'Dear Sir or Madam'.

* Another useful way to make the letter more personal is to write by hand what can safely be written by hand – the date, the salutation, the sign off (Yours sincerely, or whatever) and, of course, your name.

- Style. You have choices to make! See the examples in the following box.

The style of application letters

Here are two ways of saying the same thing in a letter to a family trust (the first being the one that was actually used):

> In the past your trust has donated generously to our organisation, for which we were most grateful. ... We have now been in existence for six years and during that time we have supported 198 families. Our main funding now comes from the Blankshire County Council Social Services Department and this has gradually increased over the years to approx. 75%. ... We now have a shortfall of £5,000 up to April next and would ask to be considered by your trust for financial help towards this shortfall ... We have recently entered into a service agreement with Social Services which we hope will eventually lead to 90% funding from them.

This is very formal. The following would generally be better:

> You helped us before in 19xx with a grant of £xxx. We are now planning to help even more families, but need your help again to do so.

> Happily, we are working towards regular 90% funding from the Council for this work and have already got the figure up to 75%.

However, to get to the next stage we need to put in another £10,000 of our own this year. Can you help us with this?

Personally, I would probably put this kind of information on a separate attachment anyway – 'The Financial Situation' or such like – rather than in my letter. Try to be simple and straightforward. Avoid jargon, long words, sentences or paragraphs. Put the detail in appendices.

Above all, if you feel strongly about the importance of what you are asking for, let this show. Trusts wish to support those who feel strongly about the worth of what they are doing, but the tone of many of the letters they get is cool to the point of glaciation.

- Appearance. You say you are wonderful, but then you would, wouldn't you? About the only thing the trust has to go on is the appearance of your letter and enclosures. It is worth a lot of effort to get a letterhead, annual reports, leaflets and so on that are unexpectedly impressive for your kind of organisation – and don't look too expensive. Quite a challenge and one that will usually only be met by a first-class graphic designer being pushed to produce his or her very best work.

What attachments should I include?

Note first that these are usually only back-up; the top letter or the summary on the application form is generally what counts most. I am regularly asked to look at 'applications' in which the actual application is missing and where I am only sent the back-up stuff.

Many trusts are quite specific about what they want. Follow their guidance carefully. Otherwise, trusts normally expect to see a copy of your most recent annual report and accounts (unless you are too new to have these yet). You may also want to add, if it seems appropriate to you, or refer to the existence of:

- evidence about the need for or effectiveness of your work;
- an independent note of endorsement from someone with no axe to grind: 'I know these people and their work, and it is wonderful' from, say, the bishop or the chair of the local bench of magistrates, or a noted celebrity;
- a business plan, especially if there are building works involved.

Caution!

I believe that most trust money (usually accounted for by a relatively small number of the bigger large awards) is given in grants to people who the trust already knows, likes and trusts, and where the written application serves largely to confirm an understanding previously arrived at in a more informal way.

Establishing such ongoing working relationships needs to be a key long-term objective for charities that expect to need trust support in the future as well as right now. However, until such a relationship is established, your application, plus perhaps one advance telephone call, is usually all there is.

Getting grants from trusts and foundations

Simon Pellew set up and ran Pecan, a highly successful charity training unemployed people in South London and now itself employing nearly 100 people. He has recently become the Chief Executive of Stepping Stones, providing accommodation and care for ex-prisoners. He took part in one of DSC's early Effective Fundraising training courses. He offers the following from his own experience:

> When I started Pecan, 14 years ago, I read through the trust directories and felt that with so much money around I would easily ... find people who would give me the money I needed to make my fantastic idea work.

> So, I produced a beautiful leaflet (at a cost of about £2,500) and a detailed description of my idea and sent it out. I got nothing back. This dented my confidence somewhat and made me suspect that there weren't hundreds of people out there just longing to give me money. I realised I would have to work at it.

> What advice would have saved me from making these painful mistakes? First, get some training. ... The DSC Effective Fundraising course's ... listing of our possible 'selling points' [see pages 18–20] opened my eyes to how to 'sell' the charity; and ... actually realising they weren't interested in my organisation, but in what we were going to do, transformed my approach.

> Secondly, don't say to yourself 'I only need one donor to give me £x thousand ...'. It doesn't work like that. No-one is likely to give you more than 50% of your costs, and probably only a

---

third. Also, don't ask for too much; if you are a new charity no trust is likely to give you more than half their average donation (this is my rule-of-thumb but it seems about right).

Thirdly, keep the asking letter short and simple. I wrote too much and I spent too much money on producing a flash leaflet. Much better to keep it very simple. Remember that these trusts get lots of applications every day. When you write your application, picture the poor person doing the initial sift through that day's pile and think how to make your letter easy for them to read and understand.

Fourth, start with a number of small, general trusts. There will probably be one or two really large trusts whose donations' criteria you fit perfectly. You really want to succeed with these and so it is better getting a bit of practice on less important trusts first. Once you start getting some money back you know you have got a reasonably good asking letter, and then you can write for the bigger sums.

One of the great joys of fundraising is opening a letter and finding a cheque. But, to experience it, you always have to remember that people need to be persuaded to be parted from their hard-earned money.

What should I do if they give me a grant?

Assume that this will be the start of a long-term relationship (or will help to continue an existing one).

- Immediately acknowledge receipt of the grant, always in writing but where appropriate, personally as well.
- Immediately cash the cheque.

It is sad how very many charities are unable to manage these elementary courtesies.

Why your funders become your partners

This does not just apply to trusts, but it is often most obvious with them. Once they have given you a grant, donors have 'bought into' your work. Your success becomes their success and any failure by you would show their judgement to have been poor – if you fail, they have been stupid. So they have a built-in interest in helping you. From the moment you get a grant or a substantial donation, you will usually be able to talk to them on a quite different basis – that of partner to partner, rather than of supplicant to funder. Indeed most trusts talk happily about the advantages to both sides of 'having a relationship' and say that this is the long-term key to successful trust fundraising. Talk to them about your hopes, fears, disappointments and ideas for the future.

I have been asked by a frustrated trust administrator, advising on the distribution to charities of millions of pounds a year, 'what can I do to stop people coming to me as if I was bank manager about to refuse a client an overdraft? Why can't they realise that I work for a charity too, that we are colleagues?' I promised then to pass the message on, as I am doing now, but I could not help thinking that there is one great difference: they have got the money and we have not. But that isn't how it seems to them. From their point of view they are helpless without us. We can actually do things; they can only sign cheques. Ongoing partnerships are not something to be created just by us; the trusts need and want them just as much.

Small grants

A grant of less than £5,000 is usually regarded in the world of the big trusts – though not of smaller ones – as a 'small grant', though most of their small grants are for a good deal less than this. In 2003, when this book was being written, such grants, especially for small charities, were easier to get than at any time in my experience. In a number of cases the success rates for such applications were over 50%, a remarkably high rate.

In general, there is some reluctance to give even these grants for regular ongoing costs such as salaries or rent. In such cases it may be best just to ask for a donation towards the cost of the work being done.

There is a list of some of the most accessible trusts making these grants published free on the DSC website (www.dsc.org.uk/charityexchange/resources). However there are many other trusts making large numbers of small grants, details of which can be found in the grant guides. Organisations often think there must be a catch, but in recent years, for example, I have encouraged organisations as varied as a group of Gilbertese dancers and my tiny local museum in Totnes to apply successfully for such grants.

If your organisation is new to fundraising from trusts, why not start off by seeking some small grants before you try for the big time? You might get some money to help with your set-up costs, to get decently designed letterheads and literature, or for some initial training to prepare yourselves for what you are getting into.

Some trusts have a simple application form, such as the excellent Lottery Awards for All programme described below. For others, all that is needed is a simple one-page letter with a copy of your annual report and accounts.

The National Lottery

Lottery money is distributed by numerous separate organisations, most of which can be accessed by at least some charities – the arts councils, the sports councils, the Heritage Lottery Fund, the New Opportunities Fund – through a wide and varied range of funding programmes. These are part of public expenditure, subject to Treasury regulation and so on, and are outside the scope of this book – and generally we call it funding rather than fundraising (you can get full information on all of them via www.lotterygoodcauses.org.uk).

There are however two distributors or programmes which are specifically aimed at meeting the needs of charities and which act so like grantmaking trusts that they deserve description here: the Community Fund and the Awards for All small grants scheme (managed on behalf of all the other distributors by the Community Fund, except in Wales and Northern Ireland where the arrangements are different).

The Community Fund

This is still officially called the National Lottery Charities Board and it gives away about £250 million in grants every year. Its mission is to help those at greatest disadvantage in society'. It has an excellent website, www.community-fund.org.uk.

The Fund is due to be merged with the New Opportunities Fund (which supports programmes chosen for it by the government) at some stage but no major changes in programmes were expected in the immediate future.

The Fund is administratively decentralised, with most applications being made to regional offices. However the rigid procedures are centrally decided with the only variation being some regionally favoured priorities and the regionally set budgets which are based on population but heavily weighted for levels of deprivation.

It has grant programmes for funding 'projects', generally to a maximum of about £250,000, and for up to three years with the possibility of a grant for a second three years to 'further develop' the work concerned.

How do I apply?

There are a detailed and lengthy application forms, with full supporting guidance. To get a preliminary idea of whether it is worth your applying, ring the development officer at your nearest regional office; they are generally helpful. All telephone numbers are on their website www.community-fund.org.uk.

The assessment system for applications, which has become extremely well known throughout the charity world, is due to be completely changed to the 'outcome funding' approach at the end of 2004 (it has already changed in Scotland).

Two cautions!

1   If your work helps everyone, including the prosperous, such as, say, a bereavement counselling service, it may be difficult to get a grant towards your work as a whole. You will probably need to have a project specifically aimed at bringing your counselling to 'those at greatest disadvantage'.

2   Experience of dealing with other Lottery distributors, such as the arts councils or the New Opportunities Fund, is of limited relevance when seeking grants from the Community Fund. They have completely separate systems and cultures. Also beware of consultants offering to prepare your application for you. If the information and detailed project planning is to hand, the application is not too hard to fill in yourselves. If it is not, expert application writing is unlikely to cover over the gaps.

Awards for All small grants

See 'Small grants' above. At the time of writing, success rates for this scheme were running between 50% and 70%. It is aimed at the smaller charity, whether registered or not, it will pay for just about anything except ongoing running costs such as salaries or rent, and it has a very simple application form. All details on www.awardsfor all.com.

7 Raising money from companies

Getting companies to give

This is usually more difficult than getting grants from trusts, so it may be best to leave it until your trust fundraising programme is fully developed, unless you have particular opportunities in this field.

Caution!

'Corporate fundraising' gets far more attention than is justified by the amount of money available. No doubt this is because, when a company is generous, it has a PR department whose job is to shout the good news from the housetops. No other source of funding has this ballyhoo behind it. If your charity is getting very little from companies, don't necessarily worry. It may be the same for most other charities in similar positions to yours.

How do companies give money to charities?

In three ways:

- in donations
- by their staff raising money for your charity
- through 'corporate sponsorship'.

Can we get donations or grants from companies?

You can ask. These grants total about £300 million a year in the UK, compared to perhaps five times as much from trusts. They come from the profits of the company which would otherwise go to its owners, the shareholders. There is always a strong argument that if these shareholders want their money to go to charity, they can give it themselves, and this limits the amount available.

Nevertheless, if there is a particular reason why a company might support you, it is always worth asking. For example:

- You may have friends among the company's staff who will support your application.

- There may be a connection between your work and the company's activities. For example a utility trying avoid bad publicity when they have to disconnect non-payers might support your money advice service.
- There may be a local connection. For example, perhaps they are a major local employer and you support their pensioners in their old age.
- The company may have a donations policy which fits what you do. For example, 'We support technical education'. So do you.

How do I ask for a donation?

If possible, personally, backed up by a simple letter, like those to trusts but much, much shorter – one or two paragraphs (you can enclose back-up materials). Unlike a trust, supporting charities is not a company's proper business. They get their living by making widgets or whatever and your letter is a distraction from this.

Who do we write to?

For very big companies, there is usually a designated procedure, set out in *The Guide to UK Company Giving*, published by DSC (www.dsc.org.uk). For local or smaller companies, or for local branches of bigger ones, I recommend a telephone call to find out who best to approach. In the absence of any other suggestions, I would usually ask for the managing director's secretary and ask for her advice (so far, it has always been a 'she').

How can we get a company to fundraise for us?

By asking. Many companies 'adopt' charities and their staff raise money for them. The company may chip in some of its own money as well. Sometimes this is just for a year or whatever, sometimes it is ongoing: 'We have always supported them'.

Corporate sponsorship

What is sponsorship?

Sponsorship is quite different, at least in principle. You do a deal with a company in which they get something valuable from you, usually publicity or PR benefits of some kind, in return for their money. The money will usually come from some kind of marketing or PR budget, rather than being a gift out of its profits.

So consider what you may have to offer a company. If they sponsor your annual report, with their name on its cover, will that be valuable positive publicity for them? At a local level, this could be the case for any business that advertises in the local paper, say. You offer them a comparable amount of publicity for a similar price.

Nationally, an association with a major charity can indeed make a company look and smell sweeter than would otherwise be the case. The biggest companies have sponsorship managers, departments and budgets. But be careful. These people are 'buyers', out to get the most good publicity for their company in return for their money and it is becoming a pretty competitive market. All too often, not much is left for the charity after it has generated all the agreed benefits for the sponsor.

Caution!

Sponsorship can sometimes be most easily had from those by whom you would least wish to be sponsored – tobacco or food companies sponsoring health charities, big polluters sponsoring environmental activities and so on. Even leaving the moral issues to you, is it worth the risk to your reputation?

How do we get sponsorship?

By suggesting that you submit a 'sponsorship proposal' setting out what you will do and what the benefits will be for the company, in return for the payment you name. Then you negotiate. Again, there is a DSC book *Finding Company Sponsors* (www.dsc.org.uk). See the box below for an example.

A theatre's sponsorship offerings

A theatre offered the following:

- sponsorship of a show for the duration of its run, credited to your company
- up to 20 complimentary dress circle tickets, with a discount of £2 on any additional tickets purchased
- a display in the theatre's foyer
- opportunities to invite cast members to attend post-event receptions
- arrangements for complimentary use of the restaurant or the Langtry Room
- name and logo on the theatre's website (www.everymantheatre.org.uk)

- tour of the theatre after the show
- publicity and PR opportunities
- print accreditation (name and logo) on
    70,000 full-colour season brochures
    1,000 season playbills
    two giant billboards outside the theatre
    production-specific posters and leaflets
    production programmes, with full-page complimentary advertisement
    press/media advertisements for the show
    press releases for the show.

For large companies, again there are listings in *The Guide to UK Company Giving*, published by DSC (www.dsc.org.uk). Locally you will just have to network.

Caution!

The high street companies get more requests than anyone else. You may get on better with other employers less in the public eye – say the big wholesaler on the industrial estate, or the clerical offices of the credit card company.

8 The activity of fundraising

What fundraisers actually do

When someone says that they spend a lot of time fundraising, this can mean a number of things.

One big distinction is between those who organise fundraising and those who actually do it. The first is often called fundraising management. It is often quite different from actually asking people for money, though many people do both. If you are not able to go out and introduce yourself to people, often strangers, and ask them to give money to your charity, do not despair. Your job can then be to organise things so that someone else, who enjoys it, does this asking.

A second distinction is between those who work mainly on paper, whose fundraising is primarily a desk job, and those who do the exact opposite, seldom putting finger to keyboard. The first may be, for example, a professional 'trust fundraiser' – there are now hundreds of such people, to the dismay of many trusts – or a dedicated direct mail marketer. The 'personal fundraiser' may spend their time talking to donors and potential donors, or with volunteers who are running fundraising events, a very different activity.

The point is that there is a need for all these activities. Unfortunately there is a tendency to get stuck in one groove. We find apparently similar charities that seek almost all their funding from trusts, or from sponsored events or from individual donors, often pretty unaware that anyone else does differently. A good example is in the disability field. For historical reasons – they were pretty much the first in the field – charities for the blind and partially sighted, especially local ones, still tend to rely almost wholly on personal donations. Indeed they may have done so since the days of Queen Victoria. Other charities, often built around media publicity for an unfortunate particular case, may live almost wholly from the income from celebrity-backed, high-publicity events. Yet more, often created through specific statutory programmes, rely wholly on public money. They all often assume that what they do is the only 'normal' practice. It is not; there are choices.

Secrets of success

There are indeed 'born' fundraisers who simply go out and ask people for money, often with spectacular and continuing success – you have probably come across one or two of them. But they are few and far between and you do not have to be one of them in order to raise lots of money.

Success come most easily to those who think carefully about the resources they have, usually in the form of the personal energy of the people committed to the cause, look at all the possible ways they could go, and then plan their fundraising to make the best of these opportunities, rather than just going off in the first direction that presents itself.

The bad news is that when I meet people later who have set out to develop their own fundraising programmes, I do find a substantial proportion for whom no money has come in. But it is nearly always for the same reason – short-term pressures have meant that they have simply not got around to putting in the fundraising time. They are probably funded by short-term grants, or by unsatisfactory service agreements with statutory agencies. They knew that this was leaving them in a vulnerable position but the pressures of coping with the day-to-day needs of their beneficiaries have overwhelmed their plans to change this situation. And then, too often, they find they have left it too late and are facing an immediate crisis that fundraising, seldom a short-term activity, cannot resolve for them in the time available.

The good news is that those who have indeed formed a reasonable fundraising plan, and then put the necessary time and resources into implementing it, nearly always succeed. I hardly ever meet people who say that they have tried asking people for money, but they said 'No'.

Indeed the US fundraiser I quoted earlier seems to me to have got it right: 'I get money when I ask for it, and the more people I ask, the more I get'.

Further reading

The Directory of Social Change aims to help voluntary and community organisations become more effective. A charity ourselves, we are the leading provider of information and training for the voluntary sector. The following selected books are available from DSC. Prices were correct at the time of going to press but may be subject to change.

To order publications, or to find our about our courses and other activities, go to www.dsc.org.uk or call 08450 77 77 07 for a free books catalogue or training guide.

Fundraising guides

The Complete Fundraising Handbook Nina Botting and Michael Norton
Ever-popular title covering fundraising principles and strategies, sources of funding and fundraising techniques.
Published in association with the Institute of Fundraising, £16.95

Successful Fundraising
Thorough guide to raising money through membership and direct marketing to individuals.
Published by Bibliotek Books, £16.95

Tried and Tested Ideas Sarah Passingham
If you are short of ideas to raise money for your group or charity, this classic text will give you inspiration.
Published by DSC, £14.95

Making fundraising applications

Writing Better Funding Applications Michael Norton and Mike Eastwood
Best-selling practical workbook to help you produce applications that get results.
Published by DSC, £14.95

Avoiding the Wastepaper Basket: A Practical Guide for Applying to Grantmaking Trusts Tim Cook
Advice from the former Clerk to the Trustees of a major charitable trust.
Published by London Voluntary Service Council, £5.50

Trust information

A Guide to the Major Trusts

An essential reference tool for all fundraisers, this three-volume series brings you in-depth research and independent comment on trusts and how they operate. For each trust, the books give grant information, contact details, exclusions and applications advice.

A Guide to the Major Trusts 2003/2004 – Volume 1 Luke FitzHerbert and Jo Wickens

Concentrates on the 300 largest trusts which together give over £1,600 million each year.
Published by DSC, £20.95

A Guide to the Major Trusts 2003/2004 – Volume 2 Alan French, Dave Griffiths and Tom Traynor

Focuses on the next 700 largest trusts which together give over £127 million each year.
Published by DSC, £20.95

A Guide to the Major Trusts 2003/2004 – Volume 3 Sarah Wiggins

Covers the next 500 UK trusts which give a combined total of over £400,000 a year.
Published by DSC, £17.95

The Welsh Funding Guide 2003/2004 Alan French, John Smyth and Tom Traynor

This bi-lingual edition provides information on funders who support Welsh causes.
Published by DSC, £16.95

A Guide to Scottish Trusts 2004/2005 John Smyth

Contains details of 350 trusts which concentrate their giving in Scotland.
Published by DSC, £17.95

Guides to Local Trusts

A Guide to Local Trusts in Greater London 2004/2005 Dave Griffiths

Details over 350 trusts which concentrate their giving on Greater London.
Published by DSC, £18.95

A Guide to Local Trusts in the South of England 2004/2005 Emma Jepson and Chris McGuire

Provides details of more than 900 trusts which concentrate their grantmaking on the South of England.
Published by DSC, £18.95